T0049513

"Keep only what you love and what makes you happy in the moment. It's like Marie Kondo, but with an added sense of the transience and futility of this mortal existence."

—*The New York Post*

"Has benefits you can enjoy while you're still very much alive . . . Could be a good way for families to discuss sensitive issues that might otherwise be hard to bring up."

—*Time*

"Pragmatic . . . The idea in this system is that we should leave behind as little as possible, or at least, not the many thousands of items of junk that Americans often accumulate."

—*W* magazine

"Even millennials will enjoy this nonmilitant approach to decluttering."

—*People*

"A mindful way to sort through your belongings throughout your life, so that your loved ones aren't burdened by a plethora of personal items after you die . . . Magnusson advises that the earlier we start the process of 'death cleaning,' the better, so we're not overwhelmed with a lifetime of objects by the time we're elderly people."

—*Better Homes and Gardens*

"I far prefer the charming, empathetic technique of Margareta Magnusson, whose book is a game changer. I highly recommend it for anyone wrestling with a lifetime of wonderful—and not so wonderful—stuff."

—Amy Dickinson, "Ask Amy"

"[With] humorous common sense, she rightly reminds readers that it takes time to downsize and that putting it off won't make it go away."

—*Booklist*

Also by Margareta Magnusson

The Gentle Art of Swedish Death Cleaning

THE SWEDISH ART OF AGING EXUBERANTLY

*Life Wisdom from Someone
Who Will (Probably) Die Before You*

Text and Drawings by
Margareta Magnusson

SCRIBNER
New York   London   Toronto   Sydney   New Delhi

Scribner
An Imprint of Simon & Schuster, Inc.
1230 Avenue of the Americas
New York, NY 10020

First Scribner hardcover edition December 2022

SCRIBNER and design are registered trademarks of The Gale Group, Inc., used
under license by Simon & Schuster, Inc., the publisher of this work.

For information about special discounts for bulk purchases, please contact Simon &
Schuster Special Sales at 1-866-506-1949 or business@simonandschuster.com.

The Simon & Schuster Speakers Bureau can bring authors to your live event. For
more information or to book an event, contact the Simon & Schuster Speakers
Bureau at 1-866-248-3049 or visit our website at www.simonspeakers.com.

Manufactured in the United States of America

1   3   5   7   9   10   8   6   4   2

Library of Congress Control Number: 2022930223

ISBN 978-1-9821-9662-2
ISBN 978-1-9821-9663-9 (ebook)

For my husband,
LARS

CONTENTS

SURROUND YOURSELF WITH THE YOUNG(ER) OR *BUSVISSLA* TO YOUR YOUNGER SELF

A lot of people past eighty complain about "today's youth." I don't. I like to have them around. They have new thoughts; they keep my brain fresh. They are a constant reminder that it is never too late to do anything, unless it really is too late (and you are dead). Until then, I still hope to tap-dance.

APPENDIX: BONUS THOUGHTS AND TIPS ON DEATH CLEANING

How to Broach One of Life's Most Important Topics with Your Loved Ones.

The World May Always Be Ending, but Spring Cleaning Always Arrives . . . Until the Day It Doesn't.

Death-Cleaning Discoveries in the Time of Covid and Answers to Other Questions I Have Received from Curious Novice Death Cleaners.

ACKNOWLEDGMENTS

PROLOGUE

The year I was born, the life expectancy for a Swedish woman was a little over sixty-six years and for a Swedish man was a little under sixty-four. My mother died at sixty-eight; she liked to follow the rules, while my father died at eighty-one—I'm sure he would have lived much longer if my mother had been there with him.

If I go by the actuarial tables, I should be long dead by now. If I go by the experience of most of my family, I'm practically a spring chicken at age eighty-six. My great-grandmother died at one hundred. Is it possible I could live for fourteen more years? It would seem so, but I think I won't. Or at least, some days, I hope I won't.

What does anyone do with one's time when one lives so long? Well, a few years back, one thing I did was write a book about a tradition we have here in Sweden. The tradition was sometimes called *döstädning*, literally in English "death cleaning," and because it is something that older women do—and society can often be very uninterested in older women's day-to-day lives—this practical, useful philosophy had not yet been noticed. So, I wrote a book called *The Gentle Art of Swedish Death Cleaning*; it came out in thirty-two countries and is aimed at all of us—even men!—who are in the latter half of life, though I have heard from a number of enterprising thirtysomethings who say they've already put the idea to work and have found it very useful, bringing calmness and order to their lives.

The idea is that we should not leave a mountain of crap behind for our loved ones to clean up when we die. Why would your family and friends want to take time out of their busy lives to clean up your mess when you clearly could have taken care of it yourself? Remember, your kids and your other loved ones may want some of your stuff when you are gone—not *all* of your stuff. So, we can help them narrow down the selection.

The book and the idea seemed to take on a life of their own once the book was published. For a year or two, I suddenly became very busy, much busier than I ever imagined I would be deep into my eighties. I found myself sitting for press interviews and answering questions about death cleaning from around the world, from Vietnam to the United Arab Emirates to Germany. I even traveled to London for the publication of the book there. In many of the interviews and articles, I was asked to show how I do my own death cleaning at home. By the time the whirl of press activity ended, I had death cleaned my little apartment so many times, I had practically nothing left!

I felt light and clearheaded. With all the stuff of my life no longer weighing on me, I began to refocus on what I would do now that I had no more death cleaning ahead.

If I end up following the footsteps of my great-grandmother, I might possibly have more than a decade of life still left to fill, so I began to look around me to see what remained, what I had in fact actually kept after all my death cleaning. I found I'd kept my memories and I now lived in a smaller, simpler way. I could actually see my life, now that there was less mental and physical clutter; I could enjoy my life more fully, even though of course there are other difficulties that come with aging.

All my life I have been an artist and a painter. Suddenly I am a writer. I like it. But it is new.

The following essays are discoveries I have made about becoming very old—some of the discoveries were hard to accept, but many of them have been rather wondrous. In thinking and writing about them, my mind wandered to often pleasant and funny memories—and some not so pleasant or fun—that I hope will entertain you and take you to places and times you may never have experienced.

Much of this book was written while all of us were caught in the lockdowns and the pandemic—when death felt very near our doors and tragically claimed so many lives the world over. And yet in writing during that time, I was forced to focus on what made each day worth living.

I didn't want to write a long book. Old people don't want to read four hundred pages—they may not live that long. But I hope this book is also for younger people, who can get some tips about what to enjoy and watch out for as their own lives grow longer. Just like death cleaning, you can never start too early in preparing yourself for and understanding the aging process, and the wonders and sorrows it will have in store for you.

In writing this book I have tried to include advice I myself needed as time marched forward, as history flapped by, as I stood in the middle of my own strange life and sometimes felt like a lonely pioneer, sometimes the happiest woman on earth, sometimes just completely clueless.

Is my advice particularly Swedish? Some of it. Are there secrets of Swedish aging? Perhaps, and perhaps I have managed to unearth a few here. What I do know is that as a nationality we are certainly not as long-lived as the famous Okinawans of Japan, but Sweden is not doing too badly. Our current life expectancy averages 81.9 years, making us the thirteenth most long-lived country on the planet. If you are expecting that the Swedish secrets I will tell you will involve jumping into the frozen North Sea to stay young or taking long saunas, like some of my fellow older Swedes do, or eating ground-up reindeer horn in your morning muesli, I will disappoint you. I can't recommend these things, particularly if your constitution is not as strong as it used to be. Besides, I am sure I would not survive a frozen swim in the North Sea and would need to be very careful not to slip and fall in the sauna.

But perhaps my advice and discoveries are "Swedish" in that as a nationality, we tend to be quite blunt, clear-eyed, and unsentimental. Aging is often difficult, but it doesn't have to be if you approach it in a way that isn't too filled with drama or with dread. And if you can find a way to make aging itself into an art, where you are creative in how you approach each day, perhaps it can be a little easier.

Finally, because death cleaning really does not ever really end until you yourself do, I've included a little appendix to tell you about a few more tips I've discovered about perfecting your death cleaning, as well as answers to a few of the most often-asked questions that came up from readers.

So, yes, while I will always recommend continuing to death clean—your loved ones will thank you—remember that the process of death cleaning is ultimately in service to two larger points: to be less afraid of the idea of death, for it comes for all of us, and to remember that after you've death cleaned, no matter how ancient you become, there are always new discoveries, new mind-sets through which to see your life and the experiences you have had. And new and familiar pleasures to be had every day—even as the final visit of Mr. (or indeed Miss!) Death approaches.

MM
September 2021

HAVE A GIN AND TONIC
WITH A FRIEND

"Hello! Are you there? Hellooo! Can you hear me? . . . There you are! Hi! So good to see you again! . . . Yes, I've mixed my gin and tonic. Can't wait to try it. *Skål*, my little Lola! Mmm, so good, but maybe a bit chilly this close to Christmas. Maybe next week we try to warm up with some gluhwein instead. . . ."

Unfortunately, my best friend, Lola, doesn't live close by me in Sweden, but in France. It's a pity. On top of that, when we were in the middle of the pandemic it was hard, well, almost impossible, to meet up. I missed her.

But then again, now that technology has given us wonders like FaceTime, Skype, Zoom, Teams, WhatsApp, and other fun things, unexpected possibilities have opened up. It's important that we who are past eighty keep up-to-date with technology; otherwise we risk missing out on so much that makes modern life both easier and more enjoyable—not to mention we don't want our children and grandchildren to think that we're too old and square to participate.

All this new technology is also good for our friendships: now Lola and I can see and talk to each other as long as we want to on WhatsApp. And have a gin and tonic—or a gluhwein—together while we're chattering away. The warm and sweet gluhwein has kept people in the Alps alive for ages—it should work for us.

Lola and I have known each other for almost eighty years. When she was eight years old, her entire family moved to Gothenburg, a town on the west coast of Sweden where my family also made its home. Lola started in second grade at the same school as me.

I remember her being tall and thin, and that she almost always wore a dark blue dress with little white dots. I myself almost always wore a sensible skirt and sweater, which probably is why I remember her much cuter, prettier dress. Not because I wanted one too; it would not have suited me— but it was perfect for Lola. I was sure I wanted to be her friend.

We went on to spend our entire school life together, even though we chose different academic focuses—I explored art and design and Lola went to secretarial school. Lola had three great kids, and I had five. When I got married, I chose a man who would have to travel the world for his profession: we lived in the United States, Singapore, Hong Kong, and Sweden of course. No matter where we ended up on the planet, Lola and I always stayed in touch.

Later she became godmother to my second son, Jan (pronounced "yohn"), something the other four kids were deeply envious of. Somehow, Lola was more of a movie star than my other friends who got to be godmothers for the rest of the brood. Lola always wore the latest fashions, had a loud voice with a special international accent, loved to dance, had amazing hair, and looked great in a party hat.

During the summers when Lola and I were growing up, many who lived in the city moved out to cottages in the countryside, where they led easier lives and inhaled fresh air into their lungs. The cottages were often off by themselves, near enough to go to the little village to buy your food and basic provisions but not very close to other people. Being so far away from the crowded city was delightful, even though you of course occasionally longed for your friends.

Our family had a house some thirty to forty kilometers outside Gothenburg. As kids, we loved being there during weekends and holidays, and so did our aunts and other relatives who often came to visit. Friends visited too, including Lola.

In the spring we usually picked flowers, especially wood anemones. Lola was a star when it came to gathering them. No one understood how she did it. She would appear with beautiful, perfect handfuls of the pretty white-and-yellow flowers. Did she grab a fistful of flowers at once, and then another? No, she picked them one by one, quickly, and with great concentration. Then, because she was a good guest with a generous heart, she gave them to my mom, who put them in vases—one large bouquet from Lola and a smaller one from me.

We still laugh at all the things we got up to back then. Up in the attic, there was a big trunk tucked away. It wasn't left alone for long once we found it. The trunk contained very old clothes—long, tattered evening gowns that no one would want to wear today, hats decorated with flowers and veils, and one of those fox skins that ladies used to carry over their shoulders, complete with tail, paws, and a flattened head. What people won't do to be fashionable. But of course we played dress-up! It was such fun and how we laughed at ourselves for the way we looked. Then we clomped downstairs in our finery and went to greet neighbors and any guests who could bear us. Mostly only my mom could.

Lola and her family's summer home was on an island in the southern archipelago of Gothenburg. You got there by one of the white steamboats that departed from the "stone pier" in Gothenburg. Today it's the site of a fancy ferry terminal and the ferryboats are now much faster. You don't really have time to have lunch on board as we did back then.

Just traveling on the steamboat for a while felt like an exciting beginning to your stay. As soon as the boat left the harbor, I could feel that salty, wonderful wind that only exists on the west coast. I was a very independent little person, or maybe the times were different. I remember taking the tram to the ferry stop and getting on the boat by myself before I was even twelve years old.

Lola and her little brother met me at the tiny island jetty and then we took our time going to their home as we wandered through the island's small village. On the way they showed me the dance hall, the tennis court, and the house where another classmate, Erik, lived.

Some days we climbed the rocks to get to Erik's, to go swimming with him and his sister in the cold North Sea or sail in their dinghy. At times, we would crush a clam with a stone and fasten it to a string. We would lower the bait into the water and lie belly down on the dock for hours waiting for the little crabs to arrive and start to feed. Then we yanked them out of the water. After, we cooked them with dill and had a crab feast.

We would catch masses of crabs each summer. To this day still, I find them delicious.

Like me, Lola also moved around to many places in the world with her husband and kids, but we always tried to keep in touch. We managed to visit each other in Mölnlycke and Nice, Brussels, and Minneapolis. Even once in Dubai!

In those days, calling someone outside Sweden or in another country than where you were was something you didn't do unless it was very important. It was simply too expensive. Sure, we could have written letters, but in between infants and moving vans it was hard to find the time to sit down, or the peace of mind to collect my thoughts. Many times, so much had happened that I didn't know at what end to begin.

But Lola and I made the effort to get together. When

you've known somebody for so long, it's very easy to pick up where you left off, even if you have not seen each other. You know each other's backgrounds and families and how everything used to be. So, it is almost as if your conversation continues on like it was never interrupted at all—you talk again about events, both happy and tragic, travels, the children, schools, new acquaintances.

Wherever we lived we tried to come back to Sweden at least once a year. Coming back felt important to me. Not that I needed to feel like I was Swedish or belonged to the country but to meet up with family and friends and hear what they had been doing the past year.

Once in a while an elderly relative might have passed during my absence. It was sad and I tried to understand it was nature's way, even though I never fully got used to the shock of coming home to find they were not around anymore.

Now that I'm over eighty, it's becoming more common for people I know to suddenly not be around anymore. And it still doesn't feel natural at all. Most of us understand that nobody lives forever, but it's still a shock when the friend I recently spoke with is suddenly no longer available. Ever. The emptiness is at once so infinite.

Memory helps us retrieve events and people we want to remember. But my closest ones are always within and next to me—I don't need to think about things we did or said. Some people just become part of you. That feels comforting.

Anyhow, now it's gin and tonic time and I've been looking forward to this moment for a whole week. It's going to be so much fun. I can hear Lola's voice, hear the ice cubes clinking in her glass:

"Do you remember when we were twelve years old and—"

"We were Scouts and learned how to tie knots and dress wounds."

"And we went to camp with big backpacks, put up tents, and made big campfires. At night we'd sit around the fire and roast bread-on-a-stick."

"They were usually more burnt than tasty, but it was very cozy and we made a lot of good friends."

We toast, have a little sip, and laugh.

"Do you remember that time we traveled to Aix-les-Bains to do a language course?"

"Almost everyone fell in love—"

"We got to know a lot of boys, but not that much French."

And so on we went, picking up where we left off, recalling memories that only we remember. Soon our drinks are gone:

"Take care of yourself. . . ."

"We'll talk again soon. . . ."

Sometimes I wonder which one of us will be the first to not answer.

THE WORLD IS
ALWAYS ENDING

Unusual times, uneasy days. I find it a bit reassuring that the paper drops through my mail slot at around four o'clock every morning. If it's a holiday, then there's no paper. I don't like holidays. Holidays used to be special days when stuff happened: family excursions, sporting events, sailing trips, swimming adventures, or even just mushroom picking in peace and quiet. Now, particularly in this pandemic era we are in, nothing happens on holidays. Not even the paper comes.

Sometimes, when it is not a holiday, I get up and peer out the window at this diligent person, going from door to door with the newspaper cart. Wondering if she feels it—that I am looking at her. Had it not been so early in the morning, I would have opened the window and shouted, "*Thank you!*"

The other day I read an article in my morning paper. A quote from actor Brad Pitt, who had played a meteorologist in a film, popped out like a knife. The article was about nature and weather, and his comment was in response to a question about what we might expect from the future. Pitt answered briefly:

"We have no future."

Unlike the North Pole these days, I froze when I read his remark. To an older person, the statement is true in many ways. Once you're past eighty, you generally don't have that much to look forward to anyway. We have to try to find something other than the future to be happy about. And once you begin to look, you realize the things to look forward to are all around you.

Like the present day, for example. I can be happy that my body feels all right today, that the sun might be shining, that a good friend agrees to go for a walk with me, and that we can enjoy all that is happening outdoors. Like when the ground becomes blue from blossoming *Scilla siberica* in early spring, the heat and greenness of summer, and come autumn the yellow leaves of the trees and the bloodred Virginia creeper trying to nestle its way onto my balcony. Oops, I'm thinking about the future now. How hard it can be to follow your own rules!

At my age you don't long for snow anymore, no matter how fun it once was to go sledding and skiing. Falling now isn't something you just jump up from, laugh about, and continue on. We mustn't and cannot fall. In the wintertime when I was a child, older people often got around in the snow by using a kick-sled. It is somewhat like a chair on a set of skies. One person sits on the chair; the other stands on the skis behind the chair and kicks the two of them along. I miss those rides. I think that for me these days kick-sledding might perhaps be ok, at least because I'd have something to hold on to.

But it still takes a lot of energy to move a kick-sled and I doubt I'd have the energy to drive a kick-sled today. I ask enough of my children already that I don't want to ask them to have to kick-sled their mother around Stockholm. Besides, kick-sleds are uncommon in the city these days. If I whizzed, or was whizzed, around in one, the people of Stockholm would no doubt laugh hysterically at me whizzing—or, more correctly, wheezing—by. Besides, I think I death cleaned my kick-sled long ago when I moved to the city from the country village where we lived before my dear Lars died.

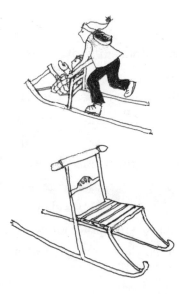

. . .

Another thing I'm happy about is my old books. I like the books of Somerset Maugham—my husband introduced me to his work. I love Gabriel García Márquez, Tove Jansson, David Sedaris, Kristina Lugn, Kazuo Ishiguro, and many more. I don't want to get rid of any of them. Many new ones get published that I should perhaps read for a first time, but instead I read my old ones for the fifth, sixth, or seventh times. They are old friends.

The computer does bring me much joy, and also irritation, when it doesn't do what I had in mind. But perhaps I can get some help with it. Maybe from a grandchild or a neighbor, or an old techie friend! The computer certainly offers more than just a way to pay the bills. I can find out everything I've been wondering about on the computer: I can search for recipes, learn everything about the history of stripes—a pattern I love to wear—find out how a menstrual cup works, or get the backstory about a new pop song I heard on the radio. I can play solitaire. I can play games, write books, listen to all kinds of music, and watch TV shows that I've missed.

To meet friends of all ages over a coffee or a good meal can be so much fun. But in the time of corona it was unfortunately not that easy to arrange, especially in the winter. We had to put on our old winter clothes and meet on the balcony or in the park.

Thank God for the phone! My kids wonder why I insist on having two phones. They don't know my secret: I sometimes use the landline to call my cell to find out where on earth I've put it.

My second phone comes in particularly handy whenever I'm put on hold:

"We will handle your call shortly. Your place in line is three hundred and fifty-seven."

Then I can leave that phone on hold while I use the other one to do something more pleasant.

At my age I also think of all the bad things that can come with technological advances. Industrialization means pollution; plastics are great at the operating table but not in the ocean. Flying makes travel so easy—but at what cost?

It makes me sad that my generation and several before it treated the earth so poorly. But I hope Brad Pitt is not right. I hope we do have a future. Sometimes on very cold, dark, lonely winter days, I give in to his alarming pessimism too . . . until I remember that the end of the world has been at hand numerous times throughout history, as well as many times in my own lifetime. Yet, miraculously, the end still hasn't occurred, even though mine soon might.

Humankind has managed to survive other pandemics. My father, Nils, who was a doctor, taught me about the Spanish flu that ravaged the planet from March 1918 through June 1920. In Sweden alone, thirty-seven thousand people died from it.

Nils was young at the time, barely thirty years old. He told us of a family that lived close to his home where the mother and a teenage daughter had fallen ill. The disease ran its course very quickly; both were dead within a week. Everyone was worried, afraid even. My father told me that special hospitals were set up since the normal ones had become overcrowded, and that they were also working feverishly at the graveyards to care for all the dead. And even with all our technological and health care advances, a century later, the world didn't manage much better with the latest pandemic. Maybe the fear isn't that there is no future, but instead that humankind will just keep repeating itself, making many of the same mistakes.

It actually feels rather remarkable that I've lived for so long given that my lifetime has coincided with world wars, catastrophes, and cataclysms. Looking back, it's a wonder I didn't die of fright. Maybe I just didn't understand the seriousness of the situations that arose. Or maybe it is that no one has the strength to be terrified for more than short periods of time. Humankind somehow continues to stagger along, surviving even the darkest times.

When World War II broke out in 1939, I was too young to understand how horrible this was. But I did notice how worried and tense my parents were. Television hadn't arrived yet, but they listened to the radio a lot. Since the radio reception was sometimes bad, we children had to remain calm and not make too much noise. It crackled and sputtered, but every now and then we could hear a man screaming—one of Hitler's speeches being broadcast. He frightened us.

During one particularly turbulent period, my sister and I were evacuated for a couple of months from Gothenburg. Gothenburg is one of Sweden's great port towns and therefore was considered a prime target. So Mom drove me and my sister inland to stay with one of her best friends, who could take us in at their family farm. It wasn't especially fun to have to leave everything at home and wave good-bye to Mom, but our evacuation to the countryside turned out to be nicer than we could have imagined.

The farm was big and well managed. The family lived off the land, selling all the produce that the animals and crops supplied them with, but all this produce required labor.

Farm work begins very early each day, but I, who had not yet turned ten, was allowed to get my sleep and wake up on my own. Breakfast was left out on the table until ten in the morning, so I was alone to pick my fill from the bread, butter, marmalade, and eggs. There was a happy-looking stuffed cloth hen on the table. If I put my hand up the buxom hen's butt, I could immediately feel the boiled eggs, still warm. Yummy!

There were many animals on the farm—cows and calves, horses, some pigs, chickens, and turkeys. It was my job to feed the turkeys. A position of great trust, I felt. They ate a goo of oats and chopped hard-boiled eggs and other things I've forgotten. The turkeys made a gurgling sound as they came hopping toward me, realizing it was dinnertime. I was afraid of them and rushed to give them their water and food. I always felt relieved when I closed the door to their enclosure behind me.

I felt more at home accompanying Mom's friend as she worked to grow white asparagus. I watched, fascinated as she would cup the sandy earth around each of the plants and how she harvested the asparagus in early summer.

Mom's friend was kind and also funny. Sometimes, after dinner, she would tell stories about the other people from the countryside. I especially remember this one: A pastor was traveling on the road when he met another carriage. The road was a bit narrow, so the pastor's driver called out to the old man traveling in the opposite direction:

"Move, you old coot; can't you see it's the pastor who's coming?"

"Why, yes," the old man said leisurely, "but the road won't get no wider because of that."

Her stories were always filled with all sorts of local people, who usually had a lot more common sense than the grand "so-and-sos" who also often showed up in the stories.

Sometimes, when the farm's workhorse wasn't working, I was allowed to ride the giant Clydesdale bareback. Even though I had not ridden horses much, he seemed to understand everything I said to him. He went where I wanted him to go. When we got back to the farmhouse and I wanted to get off, he halted gently.

And yet, far away out somewhere else in the world, the bombs fell and gas flooded the chambers.

I couldn't know it at the time, but when I think back to it now it seems unbelievable that the extreme horrors and the simple joys of the world can exist simultaneously.

But I wasn't completely oblivious to what was going on. When we got back to Gothenburg, we couldn't help but learn more, as we heard our dad and mom discussing that day's events over the dinner table. For months it seemed as if the world might end any day.

I will never forget May 7 when we understood there would again be peace. Everyone went crazy with relief and joy. There was great commotion on the street outside our house. Of course I wanted to go out to look and take part. To my great surprise that day, nobody stopped me.

Out on the main street, Kungsportsavenyn, there were tons of people singing and shouting and making noise. From the windows they were waving flags, scarves, and handkerchiefs. Some people even emptied their trash bins out the windows so that the air was full of whirling pieces of paper. Had I wanted to go home, it would have been difficult because the streets were so crowded. There wasn't much else I could do, so I followed along with the people. Everybody was pushing toward the main square, Götaplatsen, which was the heart of the city and where there would be speeches and singing.

I had never seen so many people gathered around the

statue of Poseidon in the city center. I biked around that statue with my friends sometimes in the evenings. The place was usually empty, but this evening we were more like packed sardines. At one point, I lifted my feet from the ground to see what would happen. I didn't fall down! It felt a bit uncomfortable to be so wedged in, but the crowd soon dissolved. I ran home and recounted everything I had experienced.

More than thirty years later, I went through the same experience in Tokyo's subway: if you lift your feet from the floor during rush hour, you don't fall down either. The unfortunate Japanese commuters around me did not appreciate my experiments.

At school, the peace sparked a lot of conversation. The teachers were kind enough to let us share our thoughts, one at a time so that everyone could hear what was on each speaker's mind.

I attended a secular school. Unlike other schools, everyone was welcome, and no kid had to wait on a bench outside the classroom because Christianity was on the curriculum. Instead we had a subject called Religious Studies and were taught just as much about Vishnu and Buddha as Jesus and the Holy Spirit.

From my neighborhood friends I learned that other schools had religious gatherings every morning, where they sang Psalms that they were then assigned to learn by heart.

At my school, it was different. We had gatherings on Saturdays. One of the teachers—or an invited guest—would tell a story from a journey they had taken or some other interesting thing they had seen. Occasionally, someone played the piano or showed slides. I still don't know any Psalms by heart.

Because of its religious tolerance, many parents who belonged to different faiths sent their children to this school. Several of my best friends were Jewish and we spent our days together. During the war, but also for a number of years after, I got notes in my mailbox warning me that I should choose my friends more carefully, telling me not to spend time with a specific few of them. Of course it made me very sad, upset, and angry, but I disregarded the anti-Semitic messages and continued to be friends with the people I chose.

In the 1970s, my husband and I lived in Maryland and in the '80s in Singapore. In Singapore, besides the local school, there was also a French, an English, and an American school. Since our children went to an American school while we were living in the States, the most reasonable thing was to continue on in that education system, even though we were living almost ten thousand miles away from America.

Soon our family was absorbed by school life. The kids participated in a bunch of American pastimes, activities such as synchronized swimming, football, and cheerleading.

My husband and I often spent entire Saturdays up in the stands, watching our sons play ball games and daughters cheer them on. Those days were long. The heat was tropical and the men in the commentator booth drank beers to cool off. All day. When the last game started around 9:00 p.m., they were usually quite tipsy. They mispronounced the names of the players, made crude but funny jokes, and commented on people they recognized in the audience:

"Look, folks, that's Terry Barns—recently discharged after painful hemorrhoid surgery. Give him a hand!"

Sometimes we were invited to accompany friends on their boat. To someone who had grown up on the coast, it was such a delight to get out on the water. We swam right off the boat, while our hostess prepared a tasty and salty curry stew with crabs and fish heads. The dish was served on leaves from a banana palm tree next to mounds of rice.

One weekend, another friend's family needed a deckhand. They were sailing their boat from Jakarta, the capital of Indonesia, on the island Java, to Singapore. Since the boat owners knew we were a family of sailors, they asked if we could help. My youngest son, Tomas, then age seventeen, was intrigued and expressed his interest. To sail on the South China Sea, among spice islands, sharks, giant jellyfish, and corals, sounded exciting. The trip would take three days.

Tomas's adventure became more of an adventure than any of us could have imagined.

The skipper had made the trip to Singapore from Java so many times that he felt completely sure of the course to take and had been sloppy about bringing all the necessary sea charts along for the trip. Two hours out of Jakarta the battery of the engine died. Unfazed, they set sail for a few hours, until suddenly the running backstay—an important part of the rigging—broke.

The skipper tried to reach out to other ships in the area, but to no avail. Because he'd forgotten the charts, the skipper realized too late that the boat had drifted into a coral atoll so narrow that it was impossible to turn around.

An anchor tied to a long rope was loaded onto a life preserver and my son Tomas swam out as far as the rope stretched and dropped the anchor down. Once it caught on the seabed, the people on the boat used a winch to pull the boat, stern first, as close to the anchor as possible. Then the anchor was pulled up, placed on the life preserver once more, and Tomas was sent to swim out again. By this process, the boat was laboriously inched backward out of the coral narrows—the procedure had to be repeated countless times until the boat was freed and could be steered bow first.

At home in Singapore, three days had passed; we had not heard a word and were becoming more and more alarmed. One of my daughters, who was deeply Christian at the time—she was ten—had the whole church praying for her big brother. She was so sad and anxious. I myself walked around with a big knot in my stomach; I couldn't think of anything but my son and at night I couldn't sleep. We could make no contact through the VHF radio. I thought the world would end.

The coast guard was alerted, since it wasn't uncommon for sailors to be attacked by pirates in the South China Sea. But the coast guard only patrolled Singaporean waters and it was very possible the boat was somewhere outside their jurisdiction. I hardly dared to imagine what else might have happened.

After another day with no word, and out of pure despair and mad with worry, my husband, Lars, rented a small plane and hired a pilot. They flew out over the islands and the sea to look for our missing son. All that blue and green must have shimmered below, but of course no one could enjoy its beauty. All my husband wanted was to find his son.

Finally, Lars spotted the boat from the air. Very slowly, it was drifting in the right direction toward Singapore, but the wind was still nonexistent, the sails flapping. Somewhat relieved, Lars and the pilot returned home and called the coast guard to give them the boat's rough location. Thankfully the boat had managed to make it into the Singaporean coast guard's realm and the coast guard was able to find them and lead them home.

The following day we welcomed the missing sailors to Singapore. The trip had taken seven days instead of the estimated three. Tomas was in good spirits; it had been the adventure of a lifetime. The world had not ended. Not for me and certainly not for him.

My husband, Lars, was incorrigible, but maybe he should have learned something from the trauma with Tomas.

Lars loved the sea, its creatures, and any sort of boat, so he would grab any opportunity to be on one.

One Christmas a year or two later, we decided to go sailing with our family along the western coast of Malaysia toward the Strait of Malacca. We had met a couple who owned a big catamaran that they invited paying customers on board for multiday sails around the South China Sea. The husband was English and served as the skipper; the wife was Thai and did the cooking. We missed our lovely family cruises around Bohuslän, on the west coast of Sweden, and decided to charter the catamaran instead of trying to make the complicated and expensive trip home to Sweden that December. At least if we stayed in Singapore for Christmas, it would be warm enough to sail.

Perhaps we should have thought it over a bit more.

We were really looking forward to spending Christmas week on board. We were lucky—the sun was shining and there was just the right amount of wind. The day before Christmas Eve we made a foray ashore onto one of the many empty islands that are dotted throughout the South China Sea. It felt nice to walk barefoot on the white, soft sand, as opposed to the hard flooring of the boat.

On the beach we found a sturdy branch and decided to make it our Christmas tree; we brought the branch aboard and dressed it with shells and corals. As we got back out to sea again, we soon noticed an approaching boat. From a distance it looked worn down, almost as if it was homemade. Smoke spewed out from its engine area. For a long while the boat followed us at a distance; then it started to creep closer and closer. It was scary.

Our skipper became more and more concerned. He reluctantly let us know that our followers might well be pirates; in the Strait of Malacca they are not the people you want to meet. Modern pirates of the South China Sea are like pirates of earlier eras: when they reach your boat, they board, cut your throat, and rob you of anything valuable.

The worried skipper fetched an object that from a distance could be mistaken for a gun. He kept it pointed toward the approaching boat. The passing minutes felt like an eternity as the boat got closer. Then suddenly the boat changed course and disappeared far out to sea, spewing smoke behind it as it went.

That day, the world did not end either.

Looking back, I realize I rarely worried for my children. Maybe I should have more. No matter where we were in the world, people have generally been kind and helpful, despite us being foreigners. And my kids have been wise, most of the time, and in their teens they generally managed to stay out of harm's way.

Singapore may sound a bit dangerous, but my kids never got into trouble. At night, I let them stay out as long as they wanted to, but they always came home at a sensible time. Their American friends, on the other hand, were always being watched and had strict rules and curfews to follow, with severe punishment if they didn't comply. Perhaps unsurprisingly, it was these tightly controlled kids who often got into the most trouble.

I have had so many worries—but the world is still here. So are my kids.

• • •

I often reminisce about that day when the war was over, the euphoria we all felt. But the joy didn't last long. The growing conflicts between the West and the East did not result in an ordinary war, but they still left decades of uneasiness hanging over us.

Nuclear war began to feel like a constant threat, something I often had to talk to my kids about. And soon more catastrophes and calamities: Chernobyl, just several hundred kilometers away, its radiation reaching Sweden's shores. Or AIDS. Or the fact that everything is carcinogenic. The world is always ending, and yet it continues to survive.

We must always hope for a sustainable future, but hope alone is not enough. Even if we ourselves may not live to see it, we mustn't be so preoccupied with living in the present that we forget to leave room for—and help prepare for—a possible future. The philosopher Kant said that at every turn and action you must ask yourself: "What if everyone did this?"—it is a good rule. It helps me figure out what is right and wrong. Imagine if we all did this? Even at my age it is not too late to start.

Then the world will never end.

DON'T LEAVE EMPTY-HANDED

A very clever woman I know—or knew, as she passed away some time ago—had a natural tidiness about her. Her name was Birgitta and she was the owner of the Gothenburg art gallery where I had my first exhibition in the late 1970s.

Birgitta's art space was a storefront with a short stairway, five steps down from the street level. People were always dropping in and out to look at her artists' works. Her space was on the main street for art galleries in Gothenburg. That street was also the main street for streetwalkers: I remember a blond woman who would come in wearing high heels, look at the art, and then walk back out again. During the day she sometimes turned up as a brunette in slippers. I didn't mind: art lovers come in all shapes and sizes. We are all a big family. She would point at a work of art and say:

"That I like."

It happened sometimes that the work she liked was mine. I was so proud. She was my favorite customer.

To the left of the entrance to Birgitta's art space there was a big table made of light brown marble looking like toasted meringue, a table around which the cultural celebrities of Gothenburg (there were not many; Gothenburg is not a big city) would gather to have coffee, drink sherry, talk art, and argue politics all through the day and night. I did not participate in the nighttime sessions—I was a square with five children—but I do know that Birgitta had a slogan she would softly shout at anyone who stood up to go to the bathroom, or to go to her little kitchen to get a snack or more sherry:

"Don't leave empty-handed [*Gå inte tomhänt*]!"

Birgitta was not instructing her guests to pluck pieces of art from the walls and take them home. She simply wanted everyone to help clean the table bit by bit as the day turned into night. Since they were going inside anyway, they could help by taking something with them. Her gentle order was simple, friendly logic. She said it to everyone, from the CEO of Volvo to the head of the Gothenburg art museum, from her interns to her artists. All were asked. Nobody protested. Everyone helped.

I saw how her slogan was very effective and so I started practicing her technique with my children at home. In no time at all it was part of our daily routine—and it wasn't just for clearing the dinner table.

I think the principle of not leaving empty-handed can be applied everywhere you go in life. If there are dirty clothes on your bedroom floor and you pass the laundry basket empty-handed, that is not clever. The pile will only get bigger. Don't leave empty-handed.

When heading out the front door, take the garbage with you. Don't leave empty-handed. When entering your house, don't step over the mail on your welcome mat—pick it up! Don't leave empty-handed.

A friend called Maria has another approach to making sure she is not overwhelmed by her things. Her rule is that if she brings anything new into her house, she must take something that she already owned out of her house—to be given away, donated, sold, or recycled. She is hard-core. At first it was just books. If she bought a book, she had to get rid of one. She felt this worked, so she applied the same to clothing, shoes, makeup, body lotion, scarves, shampoo, aspirin. Yes, even food.

These days her cupboards are tidy, as are her closets, bookshelves, and bathroom. There are no stacks of things that need to be sorted or shelved. Nothing just sits around and collects dust. Sometimes she even gets rid of things without having acquired anything new. That is where we all need to be.

The more I've thought about it, the more I realize that Birgitta's simple saying could apply to almost any situation in life. Sure, as I've said before, when you leave earth make sure there is not a bunch of your crap still here for someone else to deal with after you go.

But also, while you are still on earth, make sure the planet itself has been a little bit picked up after before you go. Difficult—yes. I am not asking you to take responsibility for everything since Ford invented the assembly line—but look around at the world you live in. What can you do?

Soon after *The Gentle Art of Swedish Death Cleaning* was published, one of my children sent me an article about a lawyer and activist named Afroz Shah, who devoted his weekends to picking up rubbish along a polluted beach in Mumbai. His dedication had inspired others and now each weekend thousands of volunteers, even celebrities and politicians, show up to clean the beach. They had picked up thousands of tons of trash. The article in *The Week* quoted him as saying, "Don't make it an event. When we clean our houses every day, do we make it an event? It's a daily affair whether we like it or not. Cleaning and protecting the environment must also be like this."

One of my children and I joked that Mr. Shah "*döstädade planeten*"—he was death cleaning the planet. And then we talked about his work seriously—everyone should be death cleaning the planet. It should be mandatory, a couple of hours a week. Almost like a military service. The planet isn't cleaning itself.

A lot of people go shopping on weekends, buying stuff wrapped in plastic that often ends up in the ocean. Mr. Shah cleans up instead. So can you. It may be the little park near your apartment building, or the beach where you swim, or the highway you drive to work. I love the American author David Sedaris, who lives in Sussex, England. Instead of just power walking to stay fit, he cleans the roadside while he walks. He has a trash picker and a garbage bag that he carries with him; he is so effective that he recently had the honor of having a garbage truck named after him.

I pick up cigarette butts from the streets around where I live. I used to be a heavy smoker and I feel a bit guilty about that, but with my walker stroller and wielding my trash picker I feel the absolution like a strong nicotine rush.

There is a young Dutch man named Boyan Slat who has devised a plan to clean up the Pacific Ocean. He is amazing; he is taking responsibility for plastic I probably threw into the water when we were out dodging pirates in the South China Sea back in the 1980s. Yes, I remember the captain taking a full bag of trash, punching holes in it with an ice pick, and heaving it into the ocean, where it sank beneath the waves. We were quite horrified. Even back then in Sweden we never threw trash into the water or left garbage in the woods; but as guests on his boat and relying on him to protect us from pirates we dared not argue. Thank goodness that Boyan Slat has started a movement at sea to clean things up.

The truth is my generation has been really horrible when it comes to pollution and has been very hard on the planet. Now very late I realize I must help clean up. Most of us are too old to head to India to clean up the beaches or pick up crap on the highway, but we are not too old to get involved. We can organize; we can influence; some of us can donate, if not money, at least time. So, I support Greta Thunberg and all the young people who are trying to save the planet. I support old people who try as well.

I would like to leave the planet with the woods looking like they did when I was a girl. I would like to see Bali surrounded by healthy coral reefs as it was when I was there in 1979. Today people on the beach collect bottle caps instead of shells—but at least cleaning up bottle caps is more constructive. A friend of mine had a daughter who visited the Gili Islands outside Lombok in Indonesia. There were a lot of beggars on the beach and few tourists gave them money. So my friend's daughter organized the beggars into groups to pick up the garbage on the beach and asked for donations to help support the cleanup mission. Presto: the sunbathers opened their wallets right away.

When I am gone I want to have helped clean up the world. I understood much too late in life that this is important. But I am not dead yet and will spend every spare minute I have to live up to Birgitta's motto.

Don't leave empty-handed—not this planet, not even your life.

Clean up after yourself as you go along.

I DIED SEVEN YEARS AGO— BUT LIVED

Most people are scared to die.

I died seven years ago and it happened so fast that I didn't even have time to be afraid.

It was early February and the Gothenburg Film Festival was going on. I traveled down from Stockholm and was so happy about it. I was going to meet up with some of my children and a few other nice people and we were all going to go to the premiere of a film made by one of my children. Afterward, I would spend the night at a friend's house.

The weather was slushy, as it often is in Gothenburg. Big, wet snowflakes turned into puddles as soon as they hit the ground.

My friend and I took a taxi from the movie premiere and went home to watch television and talk some, but as soon as we got in the door I immediately sensed that something was very wrong. It was as if all my strength had disappeared. I told my friend I felt a little off and would go to bed early. I managed to undress, slip into my nightgown, and get to bed. Then I wasn't there anymore. It happened that fast! My friend only knew because she passed my room and saw that I had not folded my clothes as neatly as I usually do.

My wise friend called an ambulance. With the help of my cell phone, she located some of my children. I have no idea how we got down in the small elevator with its ancient gate. I don't remember any of it, but very quickly we were on our way to nearby Sahlgrenska University Hospital, where they admitted me right away. I was unconscious the whole time and didn't know or feel anything. Those hours are like a parenthesis in the midst of my life.

All of this probably took an hour. When I woke up, I found myself in a very bright, yet small, room with a smiling young woman beside me who was soon joined by a similarly smiling young man, both intensive care nurses.

They said hello and joyously welcomed me back to the world. It all seemed so improbable, but their joy was infectious. Soon we were talking and laughing together. If these young people hadn't worked so hard at bringing me back to life, I would still have been unconscious and eventually dead. And I wouldn't even have noticed. It had all happened so fast.

Slowly, slowly, it dawned on me that I had just gotten my life back.

"Did you see any angels?" "Did you see any light at the end of the tunnel?"

These are questions I've been asked many times since. My answer was "No," which seems to disappoint some of my questioners. I really hadn't expected my answer to be "No" either—if I ever survived death, I don't know what I expected, but what I got was: nothing!

The truth was simply that it was as if someone had flipped the on-off switch. I know that many people believe they will meet their friends and loved ones once they are dead. I don't, although I can see how that would be a comforting, positive thought. Maybe I'm not a big believer in seeing life from only the positive, from only one side. Perhaps also I am a bit too Swedish and practical minded; when I think of an "over there" where we are going to meet our friends and loved ones again, wouldn't we also have to meet all our enemies there too? No thanks. Not for me. I think that when it's over, it's over.

By contrast, as I sat in that bright little room with those two young people's bright, warm faces, I felt very happy. I existed. Again.

Within an hour or two, my two beaming companions brought me up to a regular, open ward. Since it was the middle of the night, we kept quiet as two other patients were already lying there asleep in the dimly lit space.

Once they had settled me, another young female nurse came and sat by my bed. I suppose she was meant to keep me awake a bit. She managed to pass the time by telling me all about her life. It wasn't tedious, just pleasant, and she had lots to tell. She was a single mom to two small boys, four and five years old, living in the small town of Alingsås, about a half hour outside Gothenburg. Soon she was going to catch the train home. Once she was home, she and her sons were going to play with LEGOs; it was Sunday after all. I didn't need any riveting stories, just listening to her talk about her everyday life was comforting and very soothing.

As morning arrived, the doctors made their rounds and

suddenly a small circle of friendly surgeons surrounded my bed. I was told a valve in my heart had burst and needed to be stitched together as soon as possible. It felt as if they had already sharpened the knives and polished the needle, so eager were they to get me into the surgical theater.

When I think about the operation I had that day it feels like I was outside myself, looking down on everything like it was a film shot from above, only perceiving the sound of running feet, doors opening and closing, and people I didn't know bending over me. I was on a rolling sea without any steady footing, with lots of nasty, tiny, brightly colored creatures hovering around me.

Eventually, the strange, muffled chaos passed and as I returned to normalcy I found my children waiting for me, surrounding me. Of course, I was so happy to see them and a few friends who had been nice enough to come by. But what havoc I had caused! Sometimes it is a bother to get old, but they all had patience with me and I was very grateful.

My experience is that when you lose a beloved friend there really is no "proper" way of dealing with it. When a person suddenly dies of, say, a heart attack or in a traffic accident, it is a terrible shock to any close relatives and loved ones. If, on the other hand, the person has been ill for a long time and has been cared for at home, it can instead feel like a relief, even if you do not want to feel that way at all. Putting your friend's needs in the front seat and your own in the back is not good for anyone in the long run, especially if their illness goes on for a long time.

The ones left mourning suffer too. As a mourner, no matter how many times you have been one before, you are never familiar with this new situation, a life without the friend who just departed. It is not until after a funeral and everything else that follows—the rituals and bureaucracies after a death—that a completely different life can begin to take shape.

My life became so empty and desolate after my husband died. He was my very best friend. We had been through so much during our almost fifty years as a couple and we had cried and laughed so many times together. We had shared each other's experiences and given each other encouragement. I know how my husband would have thought about many difficult issues, how he would have acted in various situations. I still think: What would Lars have done now? I miss him terribly, but I feel him with me all the time. I even ask him for advice now and then. I carry our life together inside me. Our thoughts, our fun, our troubles, are all treasures that no one can ever take from me.

I was born in Gothenburg. I died there once. But since Gothenburg wasn't my place of residence, I had to be transferred by plane to Stockholm, where I was registered. While the benefits of Sweden's national health care system are many, in order for it to run smoothly they do have a lot of processes and systems by which we all must abide.

A female nurse, a pilot, and me on my rolling gurney took off in a small plane. I had my head against a tiny window and could see everything that was happening outside, even though the weather was foggy and not especially good. The nurse told me that they had already made one patient transport earlier that day and that after they had dropped me off, there was another waiting to be collected in the north of Sweden. No rest for them!

The rain was pouring down when we landed. The drops felt good on my face, but then someone stuck an umbrella over me. Christ, how crappy it is not to be able to decide anything for yourself, or do anything on your own. Only having to be grateful for the care your caregivers give all the time. Which I really was, no question.

Swedish health care is amazing; all this was almost free, though of course in truth I had paid my taxes toward it for a very long time. So, I decided not to feel guilty, though I did wish I had felt more of that soothing rain on my parched face.

At Karolinska University Hospital outside Stockholm, I asked for a small radio that I listened to under the covers so as not to disturb anyone when I could not sleep. On the hour, every hour, I heard the chime for the news. I listened intently for that chime to make sure I was really alive: each time it sounded I knew that I was.

Almost as quickly as my downward spiral happened, everything progressed back to normal. I was home again, without even having to think about it. I was summoned daily for physiotherapy: a date had been made for a check-in with the doctors. All my appointments and instructions were waiting for me in the mailbox when I got home. All I had to do was get out my diary and mark down the dates.

Well, not really! I was moving more slowly and was much less mobile, so just getting to the building where the physiotherapy took place seemed to take all morning, and getting back seemed to take all afternoon.

Once I got to the building, the hallways seemed to go on for miles, while picking the right elevator was a feat. I found it so tiring that some days I wished I had never woken up in that intensive care unit.

The physiotherapy, once I got there, was so great it was worth all the hassle. I could feel myself getting stronger after every visit, not something you are used to at my age, when every day is usually about getting weaker. I almost felt young again, or at least at some younger age where each day meant health. I truly missed going there when it was over. I learned something I had never really known before: when you are in rehab after heart surgery there is no point in trying to feel comfortable and there is absolutely no point in complaining. You just have to do the work—however painful it might be.

When you are my age, you will probably meet people who are scared to die. I have been to the hospital so many times and visited friends and family who no longer can get out of bed or care for themselves that I think we should not be scared of death but of living too long. When death comes, just hope it is quick. Take it from me, someone who lived through death, it does not have to be unpleasant at all.

VOLUNTEER AS MUCH AS YOU CAN

After my husband passed away, I cleaned out our house and moved from a small fishing village on an island on Sweden's west coast to a two-room apartment in our capital city of Stockholm.

I had few friends in the area, and having retired I didn't have much to do during the day. I kept myself busy every way I could think of. I bought a leather jacket that I thought looked good. I joined social media; I started a blog about art. After many years on an island I was in a deep need for culture, so when I hit Stockholm I went to art galleries all the time, attended concerts, hosted lunches, and tried to help people my age who were not as mobile as I. Above all, I volunteered to take care of the garden in the co-op I had moved into. I love gardening and have learned that it really doesn't matter whose garden it is—as long as I have access and can see stuff grow, I am happy. And volunteering is great fun too.

Volunteering makes you feel useful and good about yourself; it was something I learned quite by surprise when I was forty and our family moved to the United States.

• • •

In our home we always ate dinner quite late. Even when the kids were little and we were still living in Sweden. We probably ate far too late for what is considered correct for children. But we kept our evening dining a secret. The children got a free hot meal in school every day, so we knew they wouldn't starve, and we believed it was important and nice that we met together each day, Dad included. The dinner table was the perfect spot, even if it might be at 8:00 p.m., God forbid.

With five children, two adults, and often a pet or two, our dinners were usually quite lively. There was a lot of talking. We had all been through a whole day's worth of experiences since we had seen one another last, and everyone wanted to share the highlights of their day.

I especially remember one autumn dinner; it must have been a Thursday since we had just finished the Norwegian seafood soup that we ate every Thursday and were about to dig into the pancakes, which the children liked quite a bit more.

In Sweden, soup (often split-pea soup with bits of pork) and pancakes is on every menu and table on Thursdays. It's a relief not to have to think about what to cook. But a bit strange too—an entire country eating the exact same thing. Also, yellow pea soup, although delicious, makes everyone farty. I wonder how much methane Sweden releases every Thursday.

I cannot remember any time I asked my children to be silent when we had dinner. The intention was that we should all talk. This particular Thursday my husband, Lars, took his spoon and clinked it against his glass, as if he were going to give a speech.

I knew what he was going to say, but the kids gaped in anticipation. Clearly, they all felt sure that something important was about to be said. It became very quiet in the room. After what felt like an eternity Lars spoke:

"This spring we will move to America."

All kinds of looks were exchanged: happiness, fear, surprise, confusion. Again it became absolutely quiet around the table as everyone considered this news. Finally, someone asked:

"Where is that?"

And then the floodgates opened as everyone thought about their own special situation and how the move would impact them. Johan, the oldest, was in high school. Jane, the youngest, was about to start first grade.

There were so many questions that needed answers:

"What is the food like?"

"Can we bring the dogs?"

"Will we see Indians? Cowboys?"

"Do they speak Swedish?"

"Do they have Scouts?"

"Do we have to go to school?"

"Will we get to drink soft drinks every day?"

"What kind of animals do they have there?"

"Will we go on a plane? A boat?"

To uproot a whole family and move them across the Atlantic is a challenge and an adventure. As our family had grown, and needed more space, we had moved and changed houses from time to time, but always within the west coast of Sweden. This move was going to be very different, a move to a different country. A new continent. A new language.

I knew my husband, Lars, was doing well at work, and that it was a big deal for him to be in charge of the US division of his company. I was proud of him, but also a bit anxious. I was just forty years old (Lars was forty-two) and it was the first time we would move our five kids so far, to what seemed like another dimension. Little did we know then that this first major move would turn out to be far from the last.

As the children chattered away in excitement around the dinner table, I wondered how my own life would change. What would I do all day when the kids were at school? Most of all I worried about my English-language skills— they were not at all as good as I wanted them to be.

Today most Swedish children speak English fairly well. They learn it in school, but it's also probably thanks to television. In Sweden, when our children were young we had just one TV channel. Whatever was on, the kids watched, no matter what language was being spoken, Finnish, French, Hungarian, English. In Sweden we subtitle everything, instead of dubbing, so most kids back then learned English from TV shows such as *Columbo*, *The Rockford Files*, and *Scooby-Doo*. Today, with hundreds of channels, Swedish kids speak English almost perfectly.

So, when we arrived in the United States in the 1970s the oldest children could, thanks to television, speak and understand English reasonably well.

Youngest Jane had not started school yet. That spring, prior to our move, Swedish television aired a program for anyone interested in learning sign language. Jane loved the show and sat in front of the TV set as if she were glued to the floor. I believe she was worried about moving to a new country and not being understood. Perhaps she thought that at least she could communicate with the deaf kids at her new school. Unfortunately, none of us knew that English sign language is different from Swedish.

When I went to school in the 1940s, I had a lovely school-mistress who taught us English. She looked a bit sullen, but if you studied her carefully you would notice that she had the friendliest eyes, filled with curiosity. Her name was Gertrud. That was not a very common name at that time. She was the first Gertrud I ever knew.

Gertrud had long hair, which she tried to keep in order with several combs that kept falling out, perhaps because she was very lively and moved around a lot. We always longed for her classes, especially those of us who had a hard time sitting still (who didn't?), because during her lessons we were allowed to move around too.

When her class started we all had to stand up next to our desks, thus forming a line. Then she asked us to walk slowly in our lines around the classroom. At the same time we softly murmured in English:

"I am,

you are,

he, she, it is,

we are,

you are,

they are!"

Gradually she encouraged us to increase our walking speed, and volume. Gertrud sat on her desk and kept pace

by waving her pointer. Sometimes she would point at someone who did not keep the pace or did something else wrong.
Such fun we had! I think she enjoyed it as much as we did,
and when the class was over we were stomping and screaming our grammar lessons. Her method really worked; her
lessons are just about the only thing I remember today from
the classes I took at school.

Learning languages isn't my strong point. This I realized
on our first day in the United States when I had to buy gas.
At that time, you did not have to leave the car to pump your
gas. You just sat behind the wheel and waited and very soon
the attendant showed up and said:

"Ma'am?"

Confusing our metric system and adapting to the American way, I said:

"Please give me forty gallons."

This is actually about 340 liters! No wonder the poor
attendant looked puzzled.

My oldest, Johan, who usually knows what to say and
when to say it, laughed out loud and explained in embar-
rassment:

"Mom, next time, just say, 'Fill it up.'"

Another time when I could not handle the language prop-
erly was when we moved into our little terrace house in
Annapolis. It was newly built; we were the first family to
live in it.

One early morning I realized that there was a large
puddle of water on our kitchen floor. I managed to get hold
of the caretaker and handyman of the terrace houses. His

name was Bob; he was a short and friendly man but always seemed to be in a great hurry.

"Please, Bob, help me; we have a large poodle under our kitchen table!"

Bob came running as fast as his legs could carry him. When he arrived, he wanted to know if he should call the dogcatcher.

I didn't have a clue what he was talking about.

A dogcatcher?

I showed Bob the poodle. And he burst out laughing.

"That, Mrs. Magnusson, is a puddle."

I have never confused the two again.

One Sunday morning a strange and rare thing happened: we woke up late and found that the entire family had nothing on the agenda. No excursions, no sports practices, no tournaments, no birthday parties or meetings to take part in.

Our home was shaping up nicely after the transatlantic move, so we were no longer stressed about unpacking boxes and settling in. My husband and I just lay in bed listening to the silence and enjoying it. For a minute.

Boys above the age of twelve sleep like stones. Deeply and perhaps forever, if you don't wake them. We had three sons; from their bedrooms there was no noise at all.

Our two daughters shared a room and we could hear their murmurs as they built a doll's house from some of the giant, now-empty moving boxes. It was a very nice project that kept them occupied for hours every day. We loved seeing how they used items that we had never seen in Sweden; a plastic tomato holder from the supermarket became a toy bed—things that seemed like trash to a normal American family were treasures to the girls. They invented new uses for empty matchboxes, pieces of textiles, bottle caps, muffin holders, pipe cleaners, and postcards.

The fuzz from the clothes dryer filter was something new and fantastic. We had never seen a clothes dryer before, and the girls made all kinds of amazing toy stuff from that lint: mattresses, cushions, wigs, anything. With the help of scissors, paper, and glue, my daughters turned out some rather nice creations. My husband and me, we also felt happy as we heard our little "angels" speaking in English to each other.

"Ah, they are learning so quickly!"

Then we heard the tones of the girls' voices changing. We could hear them getting annoyed with each other. Our little angels became louder and louder, almost aggressive. Then, suddenly, there were not enough words in their new English vocabulary. I knew the new language certainly had a lot of bad words and insults—my daughters had just not learned them yet. So they switched back to Swedish now and started yelling stuff like: "*Dumbom* [blockhead]*!*," "*Gris* [pig]*!*", "*Jävla skitunge* [damn brat]*!*"

For just a second my husband and I thought, How will this end? What will happen when American kids start picking on our daughters? How will they defend themselves? Should we teach the little girls how to curse and insult each other in English?

We didn't have to worry long, though: pretty soon our lovely little "angels" had mouths like sailors. I will not quote them here, but Lars and I laughed at their sturdy new language. They would be safe at school.

• • •

We are a big family, but I think, out of all of us, learning English was hardest for me. I made many mistakes and our children were quite amused by my linguistic somersaults. Sometimes, though, I think it could also be a bit embarrassing for them.

It was Sunday; Tomas had his birthday party. I think he was turning fourteen. It was a lovely sunny, but cold, winter day. All the children, his siblings and friends, were skating on the creek near our house. We prepared hot chocolate with whipped cream and cinnamon rolls for them, and when they came back to the house everybody was quite hungry and red cheeked. When they had taken the edge off their hunger there was still time to dance in their winter socks for a while before the party was over.

Most of the guests lived fairly close and could walk home, but the son of the headmaster of the school Tomas attended, who was one of his best friends, lived too far away to walk, so the headmaster came to pick up his son. When he arrived, he politely knocked at our door. At that time both parents and children had great respect for teachers and especially for headmasters, and no one wanted to look foolish around them.

Of course wanting to be welcoming, I offered him my Swedish cinnamon rolls.

As he munched, I asked the headmaster:

"How do you like my buns?"

The kids tried not to explode into laughter, but their stifled giggles made me suddenly embarrassed. Tom looked mortified.

Without missing a beat, the headmaster smiled in a friendly way and said:

"Mrs. Magnusson, your cinnamon rolls are really delicious."

When you move to a new place it takes a while before you discover what it offers that can amuse your children, to keep them occupied when they want to do something other than going to school or doing their homework. Our boys quickly discovered that we lived quite near two cinemas and whenever they had free time they always wanted to go there.

One time Tom invited out a girl from another grade. She was one of the daughters of Jane's beloved schoolteacher and Tom wanted this girl to join him to see a movie starring Peter Sellers. It was *The Return of the Pink Panther*. What Tom did not know was that in the United States at that time some parents still expected that if you invited a girl out you also had to bring a chaperone. I was asked by the girl's parents if their daughter would be chaperoned, so of course I promised to go with the children. I thought it was a little bit strict.

Anyway, I had already seen this movie and loved it. Therefore, I could not keep myself from starting to laugh long before every joke started. There are a couple of scenes that are so funny I can barely even write about them now, fifty years later. Can you imagine what I sounded like in that movie theater, guffawing loudly, tears flowing, bent over from laughing cramps? I was a mess. Not only had I asked his headmaster if he liked my buns, but now I was sitting a few feet from the girl Tom was trying to impress and I was laughing like a madwoman. Poor Tom.

I didn't get any more chaperoning jobs.

One day I noticed that one of the nearby cinemas was showing a movie that I felt sure that everyone in my crowd of children could enjoy, despite their different ages.

The title was *Alice in Wonderland*. I had read Lewis Carroll's wonderful book at least two times and loved it. Our family trooped over to the theater. I got in the ticket line while my kids played on the sidewalk.

The line in front of the box office looked a bit different from what I had expected. Not a single child. Mostly single men. And the line was long.

When I finally reached the ticket counter the seller said in a very discreet, low voice, almost a whisper:

"Ma'am, I am very sorry to inform you that I doubt your children will appreciate this version of *Alice in Wonderland*."

When I looked more carefully at the advertisement on the wall beside the counter, I realized that all the actors in the film seemed to be naked. And in bed with one another.

"Come along, children! It is sold out."

I took them to see *Bambi* instead. Not the pornographic version. I thought my children had forgotten about the incident—but they show no mercy. They still talk about *Alice in Wonderland* today, almost fifty years later.

Time passed. My English wasn't getting any better. Not having a work permit, I stayed at home by myself all day, painting, cleaning house, gardening. In many ways they were wonderful days.

When the kids came home from school, we spoke Swedish. When my husband came home—more Swedish. The aerobics class I went to in the late mornings wasn't made for conversation: What should I say to the woman jumping around next to me?:

Nice leg warmers?

These women were there to work out, not chat with a random Swedish woman with awful pronunciation and no vocabulary.

I racked my brain and then finally realized that to improve my English and learn more about American culture, I should start volunteering.

In the 1970s, in Annapolis, our three youngest children went to a school that encouraged parents and friends to help with different school tasks if they had spare time or if they had special skills they wanted to share.

I shouldn't have been surprised they sought help, as the school itself was housed in a number of more or less dilapidated but adjoining farmhouses, which needed constant work.

Parents who were carpenters could repair broken chairs, door handles, or windows that were hard to open. Artist parents painted the kindergarten building with wild animals and characters from children's books. Some parents serviced the typewriters and others organized bake sales, parties, and after-school classes. The list of things that needed care was endless. It was a warm and kind community.

Every Monday, I volunteered to take care of the school's library for the younger children. Not all human beings look forward to Monday mornings, but I sure did. This was a lovely way to start the week. I so enjoyed being together with these small creatures. They were always so friendly, curious, and full of energy. Even better was that their energy was very contagious. I, too, felt energized when the day was done.

Sometimes when they were not feeling friendly or curious or full of energy, they just needed to be comforted. Maybe they would come sit on my lap for a while and talk.

This library was a simple and cozy room entirely painted light blue. All the tiny chairs that furnished the room were light blue too, and the table had such short legs that we could use it even if we were sitting directly on the floor, which we sometimes did when there weren't enough chairs to go around (probably because some carpenter parent had taken them away to be fixed!).

The first to arrive at my Monday library session were the third graders. They took care of themselves quite well, which gave me time to reset the library stamp with the proper date, pre-stamp all the little library cards, and even drink a cup of coffee before the first and second graders arrived. They were all so sweet and full of enthusiasm. Some of them knew exactly which book they wanted to borrow, but unfortunately, they did not know the title of the book. Nor did they remember the name of the author. It could be quite tricky.

Sometimes they put their chubby little hands on my arm and tried to explain and explain and explain. Some were a bit anxious and had forgotten their books at home, while a cocky little boy who had already chosen his new book and had it stamped started to climb the shelves.

When all the children had chosen their books and had them stamped, I would read them a story. Just a short one. But even if the story was short, it seemed almost impossible to get to the end of it. Everyone wanted to tell their own stories of the similar things happening to them. Very often the children's own stories were so fantastical that any need I had for imaginative stories or fairy tales was satisfied. Or at least until the next Monday.

A little girl told us about when her dad knocked down her granny with his car in the garage. Another little girl was very proud to tell us how she helped her mother buy a bra that was bigger than the little girl's head. And another told us how her dog recently gave birth to nine puppies and how much work this meant for her and the whole family. Hers was one of the stories that got the most reactions: her classmates had so many questions, and everyone wanted a puppy of course. The children's stories used such simple words that I could follow them easily and offentimes I even learned a few new words, thus expanding my vocabulary.

But these happy and instructive moments would soon come to an end, as it was time to close the blue library again after yet another wonderful Monday.

"Thank you, Mrs. Magnusson, thank you," said the children.

Someone added:

"Mrs. Magnusson, you have such a funny accent!"

Then they ran away to other important activities and the little blue library became very quiet again.

I sighed with relief when the children had left: my daughter was one of those students in the first grade class. I was grateful for every Monday that passed without her proudly telling her classmates how I had taken her and her siblings to watch a porn film.

I still continue to volunteer, here and there, and have been doing so ever since Annapolis.

In Singapore, where we moved in the late 1970s, I painted sets for high-school theater productions and for the elaborate synchronized swimming shows the school put on there. It was so much fun, but it was hard work. Just try dragging around a life-sized replica of a gilded Chinese temple in ninety-three degrees of humid tropical heat. In Singapore, at that time, there were a lot of poor families, so we organized food drives and collected cans of food and bags of rice to distribute. When boat people started arriving from Pol Pot's gruesome war in Cambodia, we gathered food for them too.

I say "we" because there were lots of women's organizations in Singapore that took pride in helping out. Many of the expatriate wives had left their jobs at home to accompany their husbands on their assignments, without work permits. Volunteering felt like a worthwhile, wonderful way to spend the days. I remember we made an international cookbook that we sold, giving all the proceeds to mothers in need.

I don't have as much energy now, but I help seniors learn how to email and use the internet. When they successfully send their first email, I see a glow in their faces that reminds me of the little blue library. Inside I feel the little-blue-library warmth too.

I understand that not everyone can afford to spend their time volunteering. We have never been very rich, but we have not been poor either—so I feel it is my duty to help out. Also, I've met so many nice people while doing it; some even became lifelong friends.

My mother-in-law was a lovely woman. But toward the end of her life she could be quite a handful at times. I remember her calling me up and complaining how lonely she was. I sympathized with her, but as I was in Annapolis, on the other side of the Atlantic from Gothenburg, there really was nothing I could do. Instead I advised her:

"Why don't you get in touch with a children's hospital or kindergarten and offer to read stories for the children?"

She never complained again.

Right now, spring is around the corner. I look out the window and long to get started with my gardening. When you are my age, it is important to fill your mind and days with stuff to do: planning, helping, thinking, and moving around as much as you can.

Unfortunately, my volunteering these days is limited to spring, summer, and autumn. So, the winter seems dull and endless. I hate it. Next winter, I have decided to start reading stories to children again.

TAKE CARE OF YOUR HAIR—
IF YOU HAVE ANY

Nobody wants to be in pain. Most people my age who are still active have, or have had, pain somewhere. Many have had knees, hips, and other bones and body parts replaced. They have labored with pain, suffered through rehab, and emerged very grateful that life has become so much easier and better afterward.

I had surgery for cataracts a couple of years ago. Before the surgery I found myself worrying a lot:

Will it hurt?

Will I have to be sedated?

What if I go blind?

Can I get to the appointment alone?

And on an entirely different level, my questions became worryingly existential:

Why am I saying "alone" instead of *on my own*? Do I feel alone? I have always enjoyed getting by on my own, haven't I?

Like a snowball rolling down a high mountain with nothing to stop it, the questions kept piling up in my head. Every thought turned into another problem, a new worry—all causing ever more anxiety.

A good friend reassured me by saying impatiently, "Get a grip! At least it's easier than having a child."

How we experience our fears is ultimately individual.

But really, I had worried unnecessarily. I got to the appointment alone, or on my own. I sat down in the waiting room, was given a sedative and some drops in the eye that needed to be fixed. That was the extent of the anesthesia. I waited for a while for it to kick in before I could go to the treatment room. There I had to lie down on an operating table while the doctor calmly and with a pleasant voice told me what he was doing:

"I'm removing the lens now."

Or:

"Now I'm putting a new one back in."

Or:

"Now I'm cutting your head off with a hedge trimmer."

The doctor now had a long beard that dragged on the floor, a little party hat from Tiffany's in sterling silver, and rotating ears. Even a little anesthesia can have a huge effect.

I kept still until he told me that he was finished and I could go sit in the waiting room again. Through the waiting-room window I saw the world slowly shift and change colors and shape. My eyesight had been slowly degrading for so long that I hadn't really noticed it. Now everything bloomed—in the middle of winter. The waiting room, the old ladies sitting across from me (no doubt waiting to meet Dr. Rotating Ears), the crisply patterned linoleum floor. The snow on the trees outside.

After about half an hour of sitting and gawking in amazement, I was allowed to go home. My vision was still a bit fuzzy; I had been warned that this was normal after the procedure. I had been told in advance that I should wear sunglasses to protect my eyes after the surgery for a few days. Even though I doubted that I risked being blinded by the dim winter light, I had dug up my finest pair of sunglasses and given them an extra polish. I was ready to catch my regular bus home and put my sunglasses on before I stepped outside. There I sat on the bus in my huge dark glasses, in the darkening afternoon, with the bright world outside. I felt like Greta Garbo—she did grow up in these parts after all! I had come and gone on my own.

Like Greta Garbo, I was happy to be alone.

When I finally got home, I noticed that all the colors in my home were different. They were stronger, deeper. A morning robe I had previously thought to be gray now had a soft purplish color—lilac. Amazing, and how exciting!

I felt compelled to walk around in my apartment and look at all my things like I hadn't seen them before. The plants, the paintings, the bookshelf, my red coat—everything seemed cleaner, fresher, yes, happier somehow. It was as if a coat of dust had been lifted. Even in the grayness of a Swedish late afternoon, all was newly vibrant to my eyes.

It felt incomprehensible that I, who had spent an entire lifetime working with colors, painting, and art, hadn't noticed that I had lost such a precious ability—the ability to see colors correctly, in all their nuances. It was a relief and a joy, as if I had been given a completely new power. I was a superheroine. "Wonder Woman" might be pushing it, but that's how I felt.

Then I went into my small bathroom and looked in the mirror. That, unfortunately, was less fun. Or rather: *it was a shock*.

In my heart I'm still twenty-five. My bad eyesight had helped me believe that, physically, I still looked fifty-five. Now came the truth: I had no idea that I had so many wrinkles! It was unpleasant at the time, but today as I write this at eighty-six, I'm even wrinklier. I am used to looking old now, and I would never trade my great new vision for the old, distorted image of myself. There are other ways of keeping young.

A lot of people seem to think that wrinkles can be fixed, but I don't think that's for me. I've seen too many people who suddenly look like they have been strapped inside a skin a couple of sizes too small, whereas others look swollen.

Plastic surgery does not make you look younger—to me it just makes you look like you have had plastic surgery. Which is fine if this is what you desire. Maybe I'll change my mind when I am 102 and my eyelids are so droopy my vision is once again impaired, but I don't think so at this point.

As she aged, my beautiful mother would look in the mirror and say, "Ugh, I'm a mess!"

And my mother-in-law used to say, "Lord, I look completely exhumed!" She who had been one of the prettiest girls in Gothenburg, with the boys lining up to ask for her hand. As she'd aged, in her eyes, my mother-in-law had come to think she had become unattractive—when in reality she hadn't. To the rest of us, a patina of warmth and a well-lived life shone visible in her face. That said, she never had surgery for her cataracts, thank God: she probably wouldn't have coped well with suddenly seeing herself as a raisin.

I feel—blessed as I am with a good head of hair—that it's more important to take care of your hair. No one's head of hair can be truly great if you are over eighty; it will have most likely thinned and lost its luster, and often lost its color too. But if you care about your appearance—which I do— then your hair is a better workplace than your face.

Most women my age cut their hair short—it is practical, I guess. And while I am all for practicality, I also must admit to some impractical vanity. While I can accept—even love—a bit my wrinkles—I don't like the shape of my face when my hair is short, so I keep mine shoulder length. It is not magic and it is some work; I comb, wash, and blow-dry it a lot. I never leave the house with "bed head." I am blessed with a good head of hair. If you are not, there are always nice wigs and dyes, masks, and conditioning treatments that can help to add interest and texture to our aging, graying hair. If you do have good hair, grow it out and look for a nice blow-dryer or curling iron. You can be old and still have nice hair, making you look lovely.

I once saw a film where a woman talked so sensibly about how much she admired the strength of her own body—but I cannot for the life of me remember the title of the film. I think about her words when contemplating my own arms and legs and everything. My thoughts go something like this: My body has borne five children, plus one who didn't live. This body has died and it has awakened. This body has sheltered me in storms and baked an unholy number of cakes. This body has laughed and planted gardens, worn gloves, and loved. I will never put a knife to it for being wrinkled.

To me when I looked in the mirror after the cataract surgery that day, many of my wrinkles were new, but everyone I knew had already seen me with them. They were more used to the way I looked than I was! No one had been unkind to me because of the way I look and I've never really been horrified by the wrinkles on others either. If others had gotten used to looking at me, then surely I could get used to looking at myself. You must get used to it, unless you depend on your looks for your career or your joy. Hinging your life on looking young is such a bad idea.

If we laugh and try to have as much fun as possible each day, we'll get laughter lines instead of bitter crow's-feet. To laugh is more important and probably more effective than taking pills that might make us happy. But of course not everyone has something to laugh happily about.

When I have difficulty on dull, dark days finding anything to laugh about, I remember one thing that always makes me choke with laughter.

A few years ago, I hosted a luncheon at my home. One of the guests was a man who used to be my teacher in art school. He had been a lot older than me then, and now he was really, really old. He brought some films from a ski trip our class had taken almost six decades before and wanted to screen them to remind us of happy memories.

He had brought his projector with him. He looked for an electrical outlet and, unfortunately, could only find a rather inaccessible one in a corner behind a curtain. As my old teacher was fixing the connection, he accidentally knocked his head against the wall and then got tangled up in the curtain and as he worked to get out of the twistings of the curtain the whole arrangement came crashing down on him with him still inside. He was unharmed, but the vision of him, a curtain ghost waving his arms to get free, had our old art-school class laughing so much that we almost forgot to watch the ski movie. Once we freed him, our teacher couldn't help laughing too.

Sometimes I wake up in the middle of the night and start laughing out loud at the memory of my art teacher, in a curtain toga. It was such a successful luncheon. I am sure that I got at least one more wrinkle from our laughing that day.

Once you have turned eighty, it's important to have the right sort of wrinkles. Even more important, though, is to start laughing early enough to spend more time laughing than frowning. If your wrinkles point upward, you will look happy instead of merely old.

TREAT LITTLE CHILDREN, BIG CHILDREN (AND GRANDCHILDREN) AS YOU WANT TO BE TREATED

Spending time with the young is good for anyone getting older; the best thing is that it gets easier: the older you get, the more and more people younger than you there are.

But within the group of younger people, perhaps my favorite is the very young, let's say children under eight. Not toddlers, but children old enough that they can at least (sort of) put sentences together.

When I was a teenager, I was determined never to have children. I do not know why; I simply thought they were annoying and whiny and completely unnecessary wastes of time. Thankfully, I changed my mind. Little did I know then that I would end up with five children and seven grandchildren.

Spending time with and talking to small children is really so fun and enriching. They have an unpredictable nature and a way of looking at things that you cannot even imagine, that you can never anticipate. Once I had small children of my own, I seemed to be surprised every day by what popped out of their mouths.

Traveling with children became a particularly enjoyable experience for me: children see everything with inexperienced, unspoiled eyes. Their comments can be unexpected and strange, and sometimes very funny.

My mother-in-law once told me about a long train journey she made with my late husband, Lars, when he was maybe four years old. At the time he looked like a little curly-haired angel. The train just kept going and going and baby Lars was terribly bored. After a long silence without anything interesting to look at, they passed a very large red barn.

In the countryside at that time, houses did not have indoor plumbing and hardly any had flushing toilets. Instead one used the outhouse, a tiny little house, always painted a special red color—*falu rödfärg*. It is a cheap paint, almost the color of bricks, which is why it became so popular. Way back in the day it was fancier to have a brick house than a wooden one. So, all wood house owners painted their houses to look like bricks.

Anyway, baby Lars had seen an outhouse before, but being a city child, he had never seen a barn. Baby Lars pointed at the barn:

"Vilket jävla stort dass!"

What a damn giant shit house!

This was 1936. My mother-in-law was mortified. She gave him an apple out of her purse to shut the little boy up. He munched and ate. After a while, the apple caused bowel movements in Lars's small body and a loud fart exploded. My mother-in-law was hugely embarrassed, but Lars didn't really know what had just happened. Over the din of the noisy train he yelled:

"Hostar stjärten?"

Is my ass coughing?

Being with my own children when they were young, I got better at knowing what they liked to do and what they were able to do.

When I had to take care of other people's children or grandchildren, it got a little trickier. Can they run on narrow bridges without falling into the water? Can they swim? They can certainly climb a tree, but can they get down when they discover how high they have climbed? Can they cross a street without causing a traffic jam?

In Sweden summer was so loved and awaited. As recently as the 1960s and '70s all kids up until maybe school age—seven years old—ran around naked all summer. No clothes, no shoes, nothing. That is, if you lived in the countryside as we did.

Today you would certainly think twice before letting your naked five-year-old out of the house, but no one thought anything of it then. In fact, people thought you were strange if you put swimsuits on your children:

"Whatever for? What have they got to hide?"

Today we put bikinis on toddlers. It is the natural thing to do.

But I remember when we moved to the United States and my younger daughter (six years old) refused at first to wear a bathing suit. As a result, she was not allowed to go in the water. It was a hot summer. She longed to swim. Finally, she agreed to wear a bikini. As she had never worn one before, she couldn't really handle the garment: the straps kept coming off; the top flopped down. She didn't care, but everyone else did. She was teased. She hated that bikini.

The year before we left for the United States, this same little girl, who loved to be naked and loved to dance, had seen a documentary on Swedish National Television that made quite the impression. It must have featured naked girls dancing. A few days later my husband and I hosted a dinner party for some important people. We were having cocktails and introducing our five children to the guests. They asked my little chubby five-year-old daughter what she wanted to be when she grew up:

"A stripper."

The guests fell apart in laughter and couldn't wait to hear the future plans of the rest of the kids. It seems all of them watched too much television—even though we just had one channel.

My son must have seen a show about people who stayed in bed all day, didn't have to do a thing, and were fed and taken care of by lovely women in uniforms. "And what do you want to be, young man?"

"A patient."

Now even my grandchildren are grown-up. They are young adults and it's so wonderful to be with them when they have time, even if they no longer blurt out funny, unexpected things. Instead I get to hear about all the exciting things they have in store. About schools, jobs, parties, hobbies, friends. And also about worries, joys, future prospects, and dreams.

So, how do you keep young people around you?

There is one very important rule—treat them as you want to be treated.

I know I have heard this somewhere before, but really.

Don't tell them about your bad knee, again. Don't guilt-trip them about not calling enough.

Just ask them questions. Listen to them. Act interested even if you are not.

Give them food and tell them to go enjoy their lives.

If you do these things, they will keep calling and visiting.

They will equate your place with a good place. Especially since their parents probably have less time than you do to talk to them.

DON'T FALL OVER
AND OTHER PRACTICAL TIPS
FOR GRACEFUL AGING

Eyes, ears, yes, all our organs, are of course worn down after their years of service. I notice I've become slower and when I make the effort to push the pace beyond my natural speed I get very tired and often have to rest a bit, which, of course, doesn't speed things up at all.

If I'm out walking and suddenly feel tired, I usually take a pause and try to find something to look at for a while: a kid in the playground making a sand castle, a tree in full flower, a magpie hopping around—just a short break to collect myself before I carry on.

I've listened to my wise children and other friends and have had thresholds, small carpets, and anything else easy to stumble or slip on removed from my apartment. Yet a couple of months ago, I fell. *Splat!* There I lay all of a sudden, facedown on the floor, without any real meaning or purpose.

Falling down did hurt, though, and I couldn't get up. Of course, I should have pushed the alarm button that was strapped to my arm, but no. This will surely pass, I thought. I will be fine by tomorrow. So, I dragged myself to my bed and managed to climb in. A few hours later, I was not feeling any better. So, I finally pushed the alarm alert button I was wearing on my wrist. In no time at all, a young man came on the line from some senior-services-alarm-button-dispatch-office. He immediately called an ambulance to come get me. And then the wait began. . . .

It seemed there were no ambulances.

One winter night when our first son, Johan, was two years old, and fast asleep, my husband and I came up with the idea to make a film for him that we would show on Christmas Eve. We decided to let the family toys have the leading roles. The title of the picture was inspired by my husband's old stuffed animal that he had saved—imaginatively called *Gammelnalle* (Old teddy bear).

The opening shot is of Gammelnalle sitting on a shelf and pondering his existence. Suddenly he sees something out of the corner of his eye, turns his head, loses his balance, and falls to the floor. *Bam!* There he lies motionless. With the help of wires and tape, my husband and I were able to make the toy truck roll across the floor at great speed to help poor old Gammelnalle. Among our pile of toys there was also a really cute stuffed animal that looked like the cocker spaniel Lady of Disney's *Lady and the Tramp*. We cast her as the nurse and with the help of string and patience we got her to help Gammelnalle onto the truck. Off they went to some imaginary hospital, offscreen, in the kitchen.

Gammelnalle perked up, became healthy, and fell in love with the nurse dog. Everything ended well. And we were laughing ourselves to death making the film into the small hours of the morning. I recall we used an early form of do-it-yourself stop-motion and that there are plenty of shots where you can catch a glimpse of us being ridiculous. We also filmed a home video of showing little Johan the film. He was very confused about all the toys moving around. We used to screen that all the time at Christmas, and Johan's younger siblings would get a big kick out of seeing their big brother toddle around looking perplexed.

I thought about this when I myself had fallen over, just like Gammelnalle, even though I did not fall in love with my nurse and my ambulance service was much better.

My fall happened during the first days of the pandemic, early March 2020. Everyone was a potential carrier of the coronavirus. Everyone could kill you with a cough. No attendants, no visits, no going inside to help an old, fallen woman. The medical world was upside down. Nobody knew a damn thing. I phoned my younger daughter, who lives in the neighborhood. She came and waited outside my front door for four hours in order to let the paramedics in.

After a short stay at the main hospital I was moved to a lovely hospital a bit outside town, deemed to be covid-free.

There were four beds separated in a giant hall, one in each corner. The staff there was extraordinary. In my fall I had fractured my pelvis in two places. I was not very mobile at all. The staff helped me take a shower and meet a physiotherapist. I was seen by a kind doctor and it felt as if I was already on the mend, but I would stay the week there to heal. I was very grateful, but suddenly another doctor changed the plan and decreed that I was to return home posthaste. Maybe other patients were on the inbound and the doctors needed the bed? They didn't tell me.

Anyway, the notice came like a shock. The comfort, security, and kindness I had known at the lovely little hospital vanished in an instant.

When I got home, they put me into my bed. I lived alone and knew I couldn't take care of myself. My younger daughter once again had to act as my nurse, even though she had very little time. She was right in the middle of a project, but still she came through. She did whatever she could, helping me and taking care of my shopping, cooking, etc., as I lay there in bed.

Have you ever tried drinking from a glass lying down? Don't. There seemed to be no straws for sale anywhere. Many stores had been hit by an "anti-plastic-think," brought on by a sudden, but very laudable, sense of care for the environment. Finally, my daughter was able to find a hamburger place that shared some of theirs.

In any case, the situation was unsustainable. I became a grumbling, complaining patient and I didn't seem to be getting any better. As I had cracked my pelvis in the fall, just getting up to go to the bathroom was a painful, lengthy process. I didn't know what to do. My daughter helped as much as she could. Of course I could have asked for medical assistance at home—but there was a pandemic. I didn't want a lot of people running around in my apartment.

A good friend of mine had been living for a long time at a rehabilitation center after surgery. It had been very expensive and was not something that even the generous Swedish national health care system covers.

My solution was to get help from Japan, the United Arab Emirates, and Portugal. What is she talking about? you may be wondering. I promise I am not an aged member of a vicious global crime syndicate.

In truth, one of the unexpected benefits of writing my book about death cleaning was that countries around the world were also interested in the idea. A surprising United Nations of publishers had bought the rights to publish my book in their countries. Each one had paid a fee to publish the book and I'd been saving what I thought of as my winnings in an account for my children to use after my death. It now seemed I would have to use that money to pay for my own upkeep before my death. I felt sorry to be spending what I hoped to pass on to them but at the same time knew that by doing so I was saving them from being exhausted looking after me.

My aforementioned daughter/nurse called the rehabilitation center to see if they would take me and help get me back on my feet. It was such a relief when they welcomed me right away. My daughter arranged the transport and helped me pack some clothes, toiletries, and medicines. Not being able to do even the simplest things is very frustrating. For everyone involved.

In the beginning, I just lay flat on my back. Everyone was very kind and caring and helped out around the clock with almost anything I needed—retrieving a dropped pill on the floor, placing a pillow under my feet, charging the cell phone, helping me drink water.

After a couple of days, I was able to go to physio-therapy. Over the years, I've met many physiotherapists. If they are making a house visit, they usually come very early in the morning when all you want to do is remain in bed and pretend you are getting better. And if you are in a hospital, you have to walk long hallways with the therapist. Back and forth, back and forth. Sometimes we get sick of these hearty army sergeants, but I came to love them and was grateful to them. They worked so hard on getting me started again. Patient and cheerful, they tell us we're doing well, even though they know we want to tell them to leave us alone. Without them we would have never recovered; without them we might have just given up and dropped dead.

I'm back at my house now, recovered, using a walker. Thankfully, I was not at the rehabilitation center too long, so perhaps there will still be a few winnings from my inter-national crime syndicate to pass on to my children.

I'm so happy with my walker, it's out and about in my home all the time. If you can believe it, sometimes I even misplace it in my two-room apartment. Then I feel anxious for a while, but at the same time I see it as progress. I mean, I must have left it in the other room because I could walk to the kitchen without it.

I've furnished my walker with a nice little basket, which more often than not is full of stuff that I plan to move from one place to another. Suddenly my small apartment can sometimes seem like a vast ocean, my little basket the cargo ship ferrying precious goods across to another continent, er, room. Though if I don't remember to always unload my cargo I may soon have yet another place to death clean: my walker basket!

The walker even has a small tray that serves as a rolling table for food and drink. Perhaps if I close my eyes I can imagine I am aboard a yacht enjoying a sunset drink and nibble with my loved ones in the South China Sea. Fending off pirates and cursing.

I call my walker Lars Harald, after my husband who is no longer with me. The walker, much like my husband was, is my support and my safety. I have a friend who, whenever she meets someone in town who has yet to see her walker, introduces it as her best friend. Another has endeavored for at least ten years to get rid of hers, continually angry over her inability to exist without it.

When I first saw my friends and contemporaries using walkers, I remember thinking it seemed unnecessary and was far too early for them to be relying on walkers. Now, after my fall, I know better!

If you are over eighty, or even if you are younger and feel a bit worried regarding your balance, you should get a walker. Because if you are over eighty, you must not fall. If you do, recovering is very hard work indeed. Save yourself the trouble.

And if you don't believe me about the value of a walker, then at least find a lovely, sturdy cane or stick that you can keep close as you wander across the sometimes-dangerous world of your living space. You never know what long curtains, or possibly even pirates, might be waiting to trip you up.

TAKE CARE OF SOMETHING EVERY DAY

We have always had animals of all kinds in our family. Cats, dogs, birds, fish, and mice. One of the boys even had a snake, when he was at college. For many years he was convinced he would become a veterinarian; these days he is instead an avid hunter, shooting wild boars all over Europe and stocking up the freezer. Animals bring joy in many different ways.

I have not been an animal owner for several years now. My home feels empty without a pet, I must admit.

But walking a dog in the pouring rain several times a day in a big city does not appeal to me. It was different when we lived in the countryside—walking around in nature was pleasant no matter the weather.

When we lived in the countryside my cats, Strimla (roughly translated as "Shred" in Swedish) and Klumpeduns ("Klutz" in Swedish), used to go with me when I went to pick up the mail a little ways down the road from our house. Or they would join me when I went out to pick mushrooms. They followed me with their tails straight up in the air.

Here in the city, an indoor cat would be nice and cozy. I would need to keep them inside, though; I can't imagine them following me down the street to the grocery with their tails in the air. I would worry they would wander off to explore and never come back. Would I have to lead them around on leashes? Cats on leashes I think are a bit bizarre.

Since living in a big city again, I have weighed the pros and cons of having another cat many times. They are very nice company, affectionate and cuddly. I've even gone so far as to think about the name that I might give this kitten. Some days I thought I might call it Caterpillar if it was a slow and fuzzy kind of cat who liked to curl up in a ball. Other days I thought I would call it Dogma if it was a more stubborn breed of kitten. Long ago I had a cat called Little Cat. When Little Cat had kittens, I kept one of them that was especially fluffy. I called her Lilla Päls—Little Fur. When Little Cat got old and died, my husband and I buried her in the shadow of a lovely pine tree in our yard. We were sad and missed her. Sadder still was her furry daughter, who curled up on her grave and lay there at length every day.

When you are older and particularly if you live alone, it is nice to have something to look after other than yourself. Even if you are in good health, looking after yourself takes so much time—you move slowly. To make your meals takes forever. Even just a simple *fika*—coffee and a sandwich or cake—takes forever to put together. Getting dressed and brushing your hair seems to take all morning, and once you have finished no one thanks you for doing it. I guess I could thank myself.

But with a pet, being kind to them, petting them, feeding them, connects you with another living being. While a pet is not likely to thank you either, they may still come to you for a cuddle. It feels good to have done something kind for something other than yourself; watching them grow and change each day is a bonus reward.

So, I have been imagining my little kitten curled up in my lap and the daily care of feeding and looking after it. In my dream, I easily forget I would have to lug the cans of food home and also clean out the kitty litter.

But in truth I can never really forget that even a little kitten would be a big responsibility. I also can't help but think about the day when I would no longer be able to take care of my cat. I'd need to arrange for someone else to give it food, water, and kindness.

I have now waited so long—and named so many imaginary kittens—that it is too late to have a kitten at all. Let's be frank—I would die before it. And even if I were not to die but just disappear for a few days to the hospital or more happily to see one of my children, what would happen? Who would look after Caterpillar?

I joke to my family about other animals I might get. Maybe a fish or an octopus? But an aquarium is a lot of work and I don't have the space. I also hear octopuses are like Houdini; if they can escape from anywhere, I am certain they can escape from an eighty-six-year-old woman who moves slowly. A hamster? A gerbil? A parrot? A parakeet? Who am I kidding? If I don't think I can look after a kitten, any other pet would be sheer insanity.

So, what can I look after and care for other than myself? I have read about care homes where old people were given little plants to look after. Apparently, the ones who had plants to look after and water every day lived longer. (When I read about this study, I wondered about the scientists who designed it—did they realize that by *not* giving some of the participants plants they were shortening their lives?)

From my own experience I agree with the findings of this study. While I have always been a gardener and still look forward to the springtime when I can get out onto the little balcony on my apartment to look after the outdoor plants, I also have a few plants by the window in my living room. Although they don't need to be watered every day, I make a daily habit of checking on them and watering them if they need it. Perhaps I prune a few branches or snip an unhappy, sickly leaf. Perhaps I even talk to my plants a little. Perhaps I tell them about the morning I have had. I notice small changes in them.

Given how slowly I sometimes move, just visiting them and watering them if they need it can take a while. I hope this doesn't sound too pathetic; I really do love the small daily habit of visiting with them and caring for them. Each day that I am alive and they are alive feels like a marvel.

Who will care for them once I am gone?

I don't know, but they are lovely plants and I feel sure someone will take them after me.

In the meantime, looking after them every day is something I look forward to. Having even a small thing to look forward to, something other than yourself to care for, is important whatever age you are.

Even if I can't have a kitten named Kathmandu, I am happy with my fern named Anni-Frid.

KEEP AN OPEN MIND

I hate it when things change.

When I was young, duvet covers had slits at the top that you could stick your hands into, grab the duvet by its corners, and easily slide it into the sheet. For some reason these slits no longer exist, and changing the duvet covers is a big hassle. Imagine if this were fifty years ago—when I had to change my family's seven duvet covers in one morning. I would have gone insane. If I purchase sheets today, I go vintage, and look for my old favorites with slits. The old kind don't have any stupid buttons either.

I love it when things change.

Just look at the sanitary napkins women use today. I am so impressed! The reusable menstrual cup is now distributed free of charge in many places, reducing garbage and making life easier for women in poor countries who can't afford pads and tampons or don't have running water. And look at today's pads! Finally, someone let a woman into the drawing room. These products are leakproof, perfumed; some are even eco-friendly and have wings. Oh, to be young again!

• • •

Although some changes are annoying, most of them are not. The important thing is to keep an open mind. The older you get, the faster things will seem to change. Faster and faster.

Even time itself seems to move faster. There is that funny phrase: "the older you get, the more it feels like breakfast comes every fifteen minutes." That gives me a laugh line, even though time passing will also give me a wrinkle.

When he was a teenager my son Tomas wanted to play the clarinet. My husband and I discussed it in detail. You do not go out and buy a clarinet every day, especially as children are fickle and might want to play the violin or the harp the next day. Also, the noise of a clarinet played by someone who is learning how to play it would no doubt be horrible. Our entire family would have to wear earplugs.

But my son was persistent and found a music shop where he could rent a clarinet. The rent would be considered an installment toward buying the instrument so that one day it would belong to him . . . if he stuck to it.

Playing a wind instrument is very difficult. Just to get any sound out at all can be very tiring. My son blew and blew and I saw his face turn blue. Finally, he and his rented clarinet produced a sound. Tomas's puppy, a basset hound named Jesper, sat beside his master and looked at him expectantly and full of terror. The sound that the clarinet made was far from beautiful. Jesper joined in and howled in pain, as if he thought he were in some jazz combo for people with no sense of pitch or musicality:

Ooouuuooauooowowo!

Jesper did this every time my son practiced. Tomas's clarinet aspirations were much worse than we had imagined. Our family had to suffer not only the sound of the clarinet but also the sound of Tomas's tortured hound.

One day when the racket was at a crescendo, I was downstairs in the kitchen preparing clam chowder, our favorite soup. Even in Maryland, we continued with our traditions and had soup and pancakes on Thursdays. I got the recipe from a nice neighbor who had brought us a giant pot of clam chowder when we arrived in Annapolis. Just to welcome us. What a nice thing to do! Clam chowder was somewhat similar to a fish soup we used to eat back in Sweden, so it was extra welcome when she brought it, as we had all been feeling a bit homesick.

Other neighbors had come with small plants or delicious cookies—at that time chocolate chip cookies were practically unknown in Sweden. They tasted like a delicacy from another world. The gifts of food helped us feel that we had friends nearby. Not at all like it is today when people really don't seem to want immigrants in their neighborhood. And not just in America. The world over.

Anyway, there I was in the kitchen stirring the chowder when I suddenly heard the strangest sound. It seemed to come from the upper regions of the house. I listened carefully. Now and then I heard the noise grow louder and then it would dim down again. I figured there must be something wrong with the pipes. To be on the safe side I called the plumber and rushed upstairs to try to locate where the noise was coming from. I held my breath and listened. It wasn't the pipes. My son had simply reached a new stage in his clarinet playing: he (and Jesper) no longer sounded like a tone-deaf music ensemble. They now sounded like the broken pipes of a haunted house. I rushed downstairs again to cancel the plumber.

My husband and I began to realize that this was perhaps what our future would sound like. Should we have a talk with Tomas, tell him this couldn't go on? Forbid him to play? No, of course not. We are open-minded; the kids must flourish. I still feel guilty; I have to admit that we perhaps didn't cheer him on like we did some of our other kids with their sudden new interests.

Needless to say, we were all quite happy when he gave up instruments and started to play American football instead. In rented football gear too. It felt almost magical to return the clarinet to the shop, released from its spell of cacophony.

Next, my daughter Ann wanted to learn how to ride a horse. She had discovered a place called Littlehales Stables not far from our house. One day she took her bicycle and went off to see if she could find someone there who could help her to realize her dream.

When a girl, almost a teenager, wants to start horse riding you can be quite sure that the idea is not going to disappear in the near future.

When Ann returned from her excursion, she was beaming. Not only did the stables have room for more riders; they also welcomed girls who wanted to use their spare time to help with the chores in the stables. If you worked hard, you could get more riding time as compensation. Ah, the beauty of free labor, the essence of America. Furthermore, her little sister would also be welcome. They had a tiny Shetland pony called Peanut that would suit the little sister well.

The little sister had never showed any interest in horses, but she was happy to go with her big sister, whom she admired deeply.

Unfortunately, little Peanut threw little Jane off right away. Maybe the pony was uncomfortable with someone on its back? Maybe Peanut was having a bad day? Maybe the saddle strap was too tight? Whatever the reason, and despite her little riding helmet, Jane got a minor concussion.

Humiliated and a little scared, I think, she never rode again.

But otherwise, Mrs. Littlehales was the perfect riding teacher. Ann loved being there, feeling more comfortable in a new country. Mrs. Littlehales taught the kids how to ride and jump but also how to take care of the horses, their harnesses and boxes. And the kids did indeed get their reward for all that free laboring—more time in the saddle.

Very soon Ann was spending all her time at the stables. She groomed and brushed and cleaned the hoofs. She braided manes. She cleaned out stables. Sometimes she was allowed to drive a small tractor to carry a bundle of hay into the stables. She was very happy with her new interest. But I worried. All the time.

Horses are so big. If they throw you off, you might break your neck, back, or leg. In the stable, a kick would damage you permanently. But I couldn't forbid my daughter from riding all those horses that she loved. But for all her teenage years, boy, did I worry about her and the horses.

In retrospect, things worked out ok. She rode with a passion for many years. Unharmed

As an adult, riding at a stable in Sweden, she was thrown off. She was unharmed, but she rides no more. The benefit is that I no longer have to worry about her riding. I am grateful.

In the seventies, the equipment, helmets, and protective gear were really substandard in many stables. Now when I look at what my granddaughter wears when riding I really appreciate the changes. On her head she wears almost a motorcycle helmet. She also wears a back brace and leg protection. Horse riding is still a dangerous hobby—but at least people seem to understand that now.

Change and progress are great in this aspect. I would never say that horse riding was better in the good old days. Instead I am a bit ashamed that my little girls were allowed to ride without proper protection. It was hard to let them go to the stables. It was hard when they came home and smelled of horse shit. But I tried to keep an open mind. Then. And now.

When we were living in Singapore, my daughter Jane wanted to join a Bible study group. Some of her classmates were already members and the group was led by the mother of one of the girls. They were a merry and friendly lot and my daughter liked them very much. I thought this could be interesting for her, especially since no one in our family had much to add on the subject of Jesus.

One day every week I drove little Jane to the study group. The girls and the mother sat at a round table. They seemed to have a very good time discussing Jesus.

After some months the Jesus mother asked me if my daughter was allowed to be christened.

I answered:

"Jane is already christened."

"Yes, but then she was just a baby and she did not get to choose to do it herself."

True and right.

So, I asked my daughter what she thought. She said that she wanted very much to be christened or baptized, as they called it. I had seen people getting baptized in a small creek when we were living in Annapolis; it looked a bit strange but not too dangerous.

The ceremony was going to take place at the home of
one of the girls; her house had a large pool. The events
were arranged almost as if the baptism were a cocktail
party—but with fruit juice. The guests all dressed nicely
for the event. We mingled and chatted. At the edge of the
pool a huge parrot with colorful plumage walked slowly
back and forth. It had a ring around its leg, and the ring
was attached to a chain that rattled. Every minute the bird
croaked:

"Hello, hello, be quiet!"

I said nothing but felt deeply that I was part of a Fellini
picture. David Lynch had not yet made his first film.

After a short while the priest, Mr. Lim, arrived accom-
panied by the others who were going to get baptized. In
Swedish the word *lim* means "glue." I mused in silence
about Mr. Glue getting stuck to things, or helpfully gluing
broken china together in his spare time with just a touch of
his sacred hand. Perhaps he was a mender of things, not just
of human souls.

Mr. Glue and the soon-to-be-baptized were dressed in
long white gowns. Together they got into the swimming
pool very slowly and carefully, all still wearing their gowns.

The fabric of their holy attire was so dense that it took some time for the air to bubble out of their clothing. For a while the group in the water looked like big white balloons.

In this solemn moment after the white balloons had sunk into the water and my daughter was dunked into it, I thought I saw her smile. Maybe she was thinking, It is not every day you get dunked in a swimming pool, by a Mr. Glue, dressed as a white balloon, with a parrot walking around it and a bunch of expat parents drinking juice and parading around in 1980s cocktail outfits. That is at least what was on my mind. Maybe it was on her mind too; she's grown up to be a woman with a surreal sense of humor, though I think less belief in Jesus than she had back then.

We said thank you and good-bye to the host and hostess, the priest, and the friends of the parrot. As an unbaptized mother, I was a bit relieved to return to my more atheistic household, though once back at the house my daughter proudly showed her siblings the new Bible she had been given. One of her brothers said:

"Great, let's throw it on the fire."

That evening when I went to Jane's room to say good night I could hear her praying:

"Dear Lord, please save my damn brother."

Today, almost fifty years later, I realize I might have

been strict when I should have been more lenient, and soft when maybe I should have been a block of concrete. It is hard to raise five kids on three different continents. Most of the time I shot from the hip, making it up as I went along. There was no guidebook to help me find my way, and yet, today, the kids are all right. My eldest is past sixty. The youngest past fifty. Perhaps I shouldn't call them kids anymore. But to me they are.

In Annapolis, my two eldest sons, Johan and Jan, did not have any time for extracurricular activities. Their days in school became longer and their hills of homework grew into Kebnekaise, the highest mountain in Sweden.

Across the street lived a nice family who had two lovely daughters who were about the same age as our boys. What a coincidence and what luck! It did not take long before their studies were diluted with movies and games. And with tea and sandwiches or cinnamon rolls in our sunken living room.

A sunken living room was something we had never seen before we came to America. For us it was difficult to explain to our Swedish friends exactly what it was. A rectangle about four by five square meters was submerged approximately eighty centimeters into our living-room floor. It was the 1970s and naturally the floor was covered with a deep shag carpet—dark brown. Imagine a baby pool drained of water and dressed in a fur coat. We threw a lot of pillows in there and tried to keep bread crumbs and popcorn out of it. It was a perfect place to relax or have fun. For teenagers it must have been heaven.

My sons sometimes helped me in the garden. One time I asked them to dig a fairly big hole where I wanted to plant a white rosebush. I do not really know what happened, but suddenly they started to quarrel. Very soon they were fighting, throwing punches and wrestling. I got scared and feared for each of them. What should I do? To intervene in the fight was not a good idea, to slug them with a rake was even worse, and to cry for help was totally out of the question. I wasn't really in danger—and what would the neighbors think when I couldn't handle my own two sons?

Sometimes you get a sudden impulse that cuts through all your garbled reasoning. My mind opened up and in one second it seemed to take in my full surroundings. I grabbed the garden hose from its loop and in seconds I was spraying my beloved sons with ice-cold water. It worked. The two separated, shocked back to reality. The three of us burst out laughing. Falling over with laughter, actually. We saw our neighbors peek at us from behind their curtains, shaking their heads. We laughed even more.

A few months later it was October 31. Daylight savings had just set in. My watch said 7:00 p.m., but it felt like 8:00 p.m., as it was so dark outside. In fact, it was pitch black. And somewhere out in that darkness we could hear children laughing and yelling.

Our doorbell had been ringing and ringing since sunset. It was Halloween and since we had never before celebrated this holiday we were all curious, excited, and a bit nervous. In Sweden, in 1975, nobody had ever heard of Halloween, and we worried that we wouldn't get it right. We so desperately wanted to fit in. Today in Sweden, it is a different story. Everyone celebrates Halloween; it is almost a national holiday. Kids knock on my door and ask for candy. People dress up and go to parties. So much can happen in only . . . forty-five years.

Back then, the people at our door were children of different sizes and ages, rigged out in costumes of all sorts of creatures and personalities. I really had to admire their inventiveness.

"Trick or treat!" they all more or less shouted when we opened the door.

We had been told to give a treat and not ask for a trick. The kids probably didn't really know any tricks. Besides, what if the trick wasn't very nice, or if the trick was very complicated and took an excruciating amount of time to complete? With a host of monsters, demons, and other oddities trooping to our door, we didn't have time for tricks. Only treats.

My sons Jan and Tom, were busy filling paper cones with sweets to give to the trick-or-treaters. In no time, they had to run to the store to buy more candy, as the first thirty-five cones they had prepared were almost gone. I guess that many children living on our street were curious to see the odd foreigners who had arrived in the neighborhood.

"Are they friends of ABBA?" Could the strangers with the funny language from another country be communists?

I don't think the hose incident on the front lawn helped our reputation much. A few nights after I had sprayed my sons with water and a few nights before Halloween we had a drive-by incident. Some drunk kids in a car threw bottles at our house and yelled:

"Fucking commies! Fucking commies, go home!"

This was 1975. Sweden was a socialist country and had been so for many years. In America at that time people were terribly afraid of communism—much like Swedes at the time were afraid of capitalism. I don't blame people for being suspicious. Some neighbors gave us soup; some didn't. Such is life.

At that time, we had our lovely basset hound called Jesper. He was forever stealing our next-door neighbor's dog's food. We overheard the neighbor complaining loudly that we had trained our "commie spy dog" to harass his fine American Chesapeake Bay retriever.

We laughed and said to ourselves:

"We wish!"

We'd never even managed to teach Jesper to sit.

While the boys gave out the candy, our girls were getting ready. I could hear them giggling.

Ann was dressed as an old man. She ran over to Judy, the girl next door, who was hard to recognize in a penguin costume. Jane and her friend Julie from across the street were dressed as conjoined twins. They wore one of my husband's huge sweaters with both their heads sticking out of the neckline. They also tied two of their legs together and got into a pair of trousers with three legs that I made from two pairs of worn-out jeans.

Today we know conjoined twins in reality often suffer terribly and this costume isn't a great idea. But this was 1975 and people thought differently. They were more afraid of communists than offending minorities. The twins moved forward with great difficulty and hobbled around the neighborhood together with another little girl dressed as a skeleton.

After a while I drove the conjoined twins and the skeleton to the governor's residence, which was located at the top of a hill in Annapolis. The governor and his wife were standing at the top of the stairs in front of the house's grand entrance giving away bags with sweets. Forty hollowed-out eerily carved and lit-up pumpkins illuminated the pathway up to the governor's porch. A spectral feast for our eyes. The whole scene looked magnificent on this very dark and spooky night.

The little skeleton squeezed my hand.

When you are over eighty, it is easy to be angry. There is new stuff all the time—new politicians, new countries, new wars, new technologies. Everything is in fact new and getting newer all the time. If you are over eighty, you have two choices—be angry or go with the flow. Please try the latter. To accept, even enjoy, the changes can be really fun.

When we were living in Singapore we were invited to a Chinese wedding. None of the kids wanted to go, but I tried to drag them along. This might be the only Chinese wedding in their lives. It wouldn't kill them. Only one came with me.

The bride was named Susan; she was a friend of mine I had met in a cooking class. For the wedding party she and her fiancé and a group of other newlyweds had booked a giant party venue, decorated in red and gold. Blushing, happy, exuberant couples in lovely Chinese silks took turns getting on the stage and being toasted by the immense crowd: "*Yam seng* [meaning "Cheers," literally Cantonese for "Drink to Victory"]*!*"

In Sweden we say "*skål*" instead of "cheers." *Skål* in Swedish is the same as "bowl." Many people want to think that *skål* is a modern word for "skull," that our ancestors the Vikings drank out of the skulls of the people they had slaughtered. This is not true. The Vikings were horrible and ruthless and did enjoy their mead, but to drink it out of a freshly chopped skull was not on the agenda. So they drank out of bowls and yelled, "*Skål* [Bowl]*!*" at one another.

In Sweden we have a number of unusual culinary delights. It seems like celebrity chefs come to our country every summer to sample *surströmming* live on camera. There is a certain moment—in August—when you open the can of *surströmming*—a rotted fish. You dress it in all kinds of condiments: onion, sour cream, wrap it in a special Swedish tortilla, and eat it in tiny bits. It is awful. Some people love it. I have tried it once. Never again.

At the Chinese wedding, we were seated at a round table

that held eight guests, a most auspicious number. We were the only non-Chinese people at the party and it felt as if we were treated with extra attention and care. There was a spinning tray in the middle of the table; with their chopsticks the six other guests at our table made sure to pick choice pieces of food from the many dishes to put on our plates, as is the custom with important guests. We certainly weren't so important, but it was lovely that they treated us as such.

In Sweden we call the fatty part by the chicken tail *gumpen*. We throw it into soup stock and don't eat it on its own. At this wedding, it was considered a prime morsel. Our table mates put the fatty little tails on our plates. We ate them dutifully. As we hoped for something else a bit more familiar to eat, they started grabbing more little tails from other tables. The *gweilo* (ghost people, i.e., us) seemed to love them.

It was a long night. It was a lovely night. It was a night of indigestion.

We were in Singapore for six years. So much happened. We had so much fun. We do not remember any night more clearly than this one, the night of chicken fat—the night of the *gumpen*—Gumpen Eve. A night we were treated like royalty.

The older I get, the more I find that I remember clearly all the things I said yes to, just when I was about to say no. I must admit I have not been open-minded all the time. I just wish I had been.

EAT CHOCOLATE

How great did hot chocolate with whipped cream taste when you were a kid? There you sat with all your friends on a snowy day or at a birthday party and you all had white cream mustaches.

Or when the family went skiing on a cold, sunny, crisp day during winter break. It was so lovely to drink a cup of hot chocolate while gliding along through the snowy woods. Skiing and sipping from a thermos: it gave you renewed strength to carry on, enough for the rest of the day.

Sometimes, at home, when my sister and I had a craving—we both had a sweet tooth—we would mix together sugar, cocoa powder, and some milk into a gooey concoction that was much too easy to finish all in one gulp. You never get too old for the taste of chocolate. I still find it deliciously tasty, but these days I much prefer it in the form of chocolate bars. Even better, you then don't have to clean up any mugs or mixing tools.

In my teens I suddenly discovered how easy it was to outgrow my clothes. I don't know if it was because I continued to eat chocolate—and anything else sweet that I could find—or it was just my hormones or the growth spurts of that age, but I began to find my continually shrinking clothes very annoying. It seemed as if every month I was asking my mother to let out the waists of my skirts or lengthen their hems. She made me do the sewing, which I didn't love to do.

After all the alterations, I began to try to eat a bit less chocolate and maybe just a little less of everything, but still I grew. I never developed anorexia or bulimia—terrible diseases that did not even have names when I was growing up—but it did lead to a lifelong sensitivity about my weight and perhaps a little too much awareness of my diet.

In my early twenties, when my future husband, Lars, started calling me *rundstycke*, I couldn't laugh along with him: where I am from *rundstycke* is the word for a bread roll, or a fluffy bun. I was determined not to be a *rundstycke*.

Pretty soon I knew the little handbook *The Calorie Guide* by heart. Maybe I'd be fine for Lars to call me something like *finsk pinne* (a long, thin cookie), but I was a bit concerned that he might not like to marry a fluffy bun.

Of course you can eat everything and lots of it, be round, beautiful, and happy. If I were a different person that might be completely fine, but wearing caftans is not my style.

Then (and now) I really liked to wear and enjoy the clothes I already had. I was also too lazy to always be using a needle and thread to readjust and alter my clothing. (In the 1940s and '50s when the world was still recovering from the world war, there were certainly not the endless amounts of cheap disposable clothes there are now.) At the same time I wanted to be able to eat well without having that stubborn little needle on the scale moving ever farther to the right.

Using *The Calorie Guide*, I discovered how I could eat my fill without outgrowing my clothes. It worked so-so, I guess. I got a bit tired of cucumbers, which, from what I understood, burned off more calories in the digestion than they returned to the body. But with *The Calorie Guide*, I did at least get better at math as I sat there at the kitchen table, trying to add up in my head all the calories I had consumed during each meal. Lars was pleased; he began to think I had a head for numbers and thus the ability to stay on top of household economies— a job I rather excelled at over the years.

After surgery a few years ago, I went to rehab to get back on my feet again. There I had the misfortune of being matched with a scratchy, rather unfriendly nurse, who thought I was much too skinny.

It was sometime after my dear Lars had died. While I didn't worry about him thinking I looked like a *rundstycke* any longer, my youthful days of cucumber salads were long gone. While skinniness certainly wasn't something I strived for—I'd long ago given away my calorie counter book, probably to a rummage sale—I had lost several kilos during my recovery from the surgery. Perhaps youthful vanity never really dies, so at first I was pleased when this nurse pointed out that I looked "skinny" . . . until she went on to say that she thought skinny elderly people look *very* gray and *very* lonely. She could have been a bit nicer, that nurse.

In the past, my friends and I used to joke that maybe the best way to keep our aging, beginning-to-sag skin taut would be to eat second helpings of food so delicious that it would both fill us up and perhaps plump up our aging lines. Reaching for another piece of cake, one of us would say:

"It will always fill out a wrinkle."

After my unfriendly nurse's comment, paying attention to what I ate was no longer a joke. Eating more became of vital importance; one does not have to be vain to not want to look *very* gray and *very* lonely.

But cooking for yourself and eating alone isn't fun. I think most people would agree with me about that. You might say the answer is to invite someone over, but it's not that easy to travel at my age, even just down the block. In our most recent, anxious times, that walk down the block to get to a meal in an enclosed space takes on a whole new terrifying meaning. Even with our current obstacles, I think that most people, even some as old as me, have found ways with particularly cautious close friends or family members to meet up on occasion, outdoors or at home. It is possible to keep a distance even at a set table and it is certainly more fun to cook up something good if you don't have to sit and eat it alone.

After I said good-bye to my unfriendly nurse and returned home, a really nice and friendly dietitian began to visit me weekly. She always brought a scale with her and she gave me no choice but to step up on it. She then ordered me to drink special nutritional weight-gaining drinks and gave me other sound dietary advice. As I put on weight, she came less and less frequently. I thought that was a good sign. I am beginning to think she may never need to come back. . . .

The hot chocolate and whipped cream of my childhood left their mark on me and the mark gets deeper the older

I am, which seems weird, given that the memory of those childhood times should get further and further away. The memory of that delicious chocolate returns to me. More and more I long for it. And these days with no calorie counter, no visiting dietitian, and no cucumber salad, my longing doesn't last very long. I just give in to it, to my desire for that chocolate.

In the months when I could not go outside, when visitors dropped my groceries outside my door, I always requested a supply of chocolate bars.

My relation to chocolate is now like in that film *Little Miss Sunshine* where Alan Arkin—bless him—plays the grandfather who starts doing heroin at age seventy-something.

What the hell, he thinks.

That is me with chocolate right now: What the hell, I think. I am eighty-six. If the chocolate doesn't kill me, something much less pleasant will.

Reaching for my chocolate bar, I think of those brave retired Japanese firemen and rescue workers who offered to enter the nuclear power plant of Fukushima after the tsunami disaster to shut it down and clean it up, even though they knew by doing so they were dooming themselves to deadly radiation poisoning.

But they thought, Let us in! We can do this! We know how to stop this disaster! We know how to make everyone safe!

They reasoned, Why make young people clean up this mess and get radiation poisoning? We are too old to die from whatever the Geiger counter says.

I guess they said, "*Nante kotta* [what the hell]*!*"
なんてこったい

While I am certainly not saying that my addiction to chocolate bars will contribute to my saving my nation from a tragedy, I do admire their spirit. When you get to be very old, sometimes there are days when all you can say is: "What the hell!"

There have been tons of studies done on the positive effect of chocolate on our circulation, heart, and brain. But chocolate is like red wine—for every study that tells you it will do good things for you, there is a competing study that tells you all the terrible things. Too much red wine causes elevated blood sugar levels, or elevated heart arrhythmia, or just getting very drunk. What the hell!

But life always seems to give you what you deserve. There is no escape: even in old age there are consequences for your decisions. My decision to eat chocolate bars as if I might live forever—or, more correctly, just no longer too concerned if I don't—seems to have earned me an allergic reaction. Now, whenever I eat my first little piece of chocolate for my daily dessert, something strange happens. I start sneezing. Sometimes aggressively—eight or nine times in quick succession.

But as soon as I stop sneezing, I reach for the next bit of chocolate. At my age it is really important to sometimes think, What the hell!

THE HABIT OF *KÄRT BESVÄR*

There's an idiom in Swedish—*kärt besvär*—that I quite love. I think it sums up many of the important things we do in life. And as one ages, it seems more and more that everything becomes a *kärt besvär* (sounds like "shairt bessvair").

The words break down to *kärt*, meaning "dear or cherished or beloved," and *besvär*, meaning "pain or sorrow," but it can also mean a burden or something that is a nuisance.

Paying your monthly bills might be considered a *kärt besvär*: they are an annoying obligation, but you are grateful that you have the money to be able to pay and can feel good crossing them off your to-do list.

Or a more heartfelt example might be looking after a sick loved one. Taking care of a sick person can be a burden, but being well enough to nurse them back to health is its own blessing, something to be cherished and something the sick person will also be thankful for, even if they never tell you.

The older I get, everything I do seems to be its own sort of burden—almost anything can now be physically or mentally difficult. There seems to be no other choice than to see each and every burden, every nuisance, every pain, as something that is also dear, something that I must find a way to cherish.

Two things that I apply my approach of *kärt besvär* to are my memory and the daily routines I stick to, to keep me sane and relatively healthy.

I'm sure it happens to all of us at some point: we think we are losing our memory or simply going crazy. Sometimes it can be that we feel we have too much to take care of, too much to do. But we can do much more—and remember much more, unless we have a terrible illness—than we believe we can. Sometimes it just takes a bit more time and patience with oneself and perhaps changing our approach.

The older we get, the more often our memories can play tricks on us. But having a good memory is wonderful, so I still try to have one. Not because I want to know train time-tables by heart, but remembering people's names is not only nice but also important. When I find myself searching to remember a name, it is a pain. When I suddenly remember it, it is a beloved joy.

I know that even by the age of forty it can become increasingly difficult to remember names. I remind myself of this often: Now that I am more than double the age of forty, why would it be so strange when I go to get something in the kitchen and once there I have forgotten what I was going to pick up? It's a bit annoying, but if I retrace my steps to where I began my journey I will soon remember what it was I was going into the kitchen to get. It was a nuisance to walk all the way back, but boy was I grateful that I remembered.

Many people claim that crossword puzzles and Sudoku are good for keeping the mind fresh. People also say bridge and other memory games force the brain to make an effort. I think those people are probably right, but I have never been very good with puzzles or card games.

But more than mental games, researchers claim that physical exercise is a must for the aging brain. Physical exercise is important not only for our general well-being but also for coping better with stress, becoming more creative, and having a better memory.

A good friend once told me that you should never sit still for more than twenty minutes at a time. This doesn't work if you like going to the cinema—unless you are going to a short-film festival.

I read somewhere that the chair is our most dangerous invention—that more people die from unhealthy conditions that are exacerbated by sitting too much than by anything else. I don't know if that is true, but I try not to sit too much. I prefer to stand or to move around as much as my walker allows. I've even found a way to make doing daily exercise fun; at around 9:00 a.m. every day I follow along with a short and light gymnastic program on television. It is certainly *kärt besvär*: sometimes I can't believe my old body can move at all and it often aches. Yet I'm so grateful that I can at least—sort of—follow along.

Too much free time on your hands? Strange new shortened sleep patterns where you wake long before sunup wondering if you actually slept at all? These are other perils of aging and challenges that are a daily battle.

The older one gets, the more one must find a way to make any routine a beloved routine, even if it is sometimes a pain.

My daily newspaper arrives every morning, then perhaps I reread books I'd forgotten I had on my bookshelves. Perhaps I imagine future hobbies I will take up. I use the phone a lot (my children can tell you . . .). I wash my clothes and my sheets and towels regularly. I keep my little apartment as tidy as possible; I am very happy my apartment is not bigger.

None of these activities are extraordinary, I know. You were expecting Swedish secrets, and yet I think the secrets of aging well and happily are in finding ways to make your routines dear to you. I may not have a choice in how long they will take me to do or whether I will even be alive a few weeks from now, but I do have the choice to decide how to approach my daily life. Most days—not all days—I'm able to see my daily routine, my daily life, as *kärt besvär*.

WEAR STRIPES

I don't know why, but there is something strange about stripes, something almost magical.

A lonely stripe can be simply a line or just a stroke of a brush. A single stripe can point us in a direction but also can be limiting, yes, even mark a stop. Several stripes together can form interesting patterns.

I love stripes. Mostly lengthways but crosswise is also ok. I feel fresh and lively if I put on a striped sweater or dress. It's a timeless fashion that suits both men and women of all ages; it's graphic and bright, but also in control.

Stripes are sporty but not so sporty that you look like you are part of some training squad for Vasaloppet. Vasaloppet is a major Swedish cross-country skiing event for the really insane; it's the oldest cross-country skiing event in the world, in which skiers traverse ninety kilometers of frozen late-winter Sweden. The race commemorates one of our kings' fleeing from an invading Danish king. I doubt either was wearing stripes: I don't think they were in vogue in 1520.

Horizontal lines are said to be calming because they echo the simplicity of the horizon; I think I agree. Vertical lines on the other hand can sometimes feel a bit more oppressive, as if a gate or an elevator door slammed shut in front of your nose. But a stripe is a stripe in any direction.

As a little child, you are happy the first time a pen leaves an imprint on a piece of paper. Perhaps you drew a line. And perhaps you soon discovered that if you drew more lines you created a house, then more lines created a stick figure who might live in your newly drawn house. Unfortunately, I don't know how that same little child feels the first time they come in contact with a computer. But of course there are other discoveries to be made there. That feels comforting at my age.

Many artists have spent the greater part of their artistic careers painting lines. Fifty-one-year-old Swedish artist Jacob Dahlgren is one of them. He thinks of himself as a living exhibition for his artistic ideas and obsession with stripes. He has worn striped T-shirts for almost fifteen years now. His collection of striped T-shirts is vast. All his art is striped—it is fascinating.

A couple of years ago, I saw one of his exhibitions at the Andréhn-Schiptjenko gallery here in Stockholm. There was so much ingenuity and joy and everything was made of stripes! One large piece (roughly two by three meters big) looked very exciting, I thought, so I moved closer to it. There I discovered it was made out of tightly clustered wooden black and white coat hangers. From a distance it looked like they were all occupying the same space. It is hard to explain. It was striped. Most of the works were in bright, clean colors, and there was so much to see and be amused by.

Jacob Dahlgren has made many public artworks around Sweden. His work is represented in several museums around the world, including the Gothenburg Museum of Art. The popularity of his work is a testament to the fact that most people really like stripes.

Not being as mobile as I used to be, I take great pleasure in going to exhibitions online and visiting an artist in their studio. When I discovered Irish-born artist Sean Scully online, at first it took some time to understand his paintings and to understand why I loved his work. His specialty is large paintings with stripes painted in muted color tones, which he sometimes repaints endlessly. The other day I virtually peeked into his studio while he was working—amazing.

These two artists are each other's opposite: one uses stripes to communicate joy and playfulness; the other conveys a heavier, sometimes even somber beauty.

Throughout the centuries, striped clothing has been both hated and loved—it's played many different roles. Football referees used to wear black and white vertical stripes and were of course always hated. Prisoners wore striped uniforms. We would rather like to forget those connotations. But I don't mind remembering the beautiful dress with broad black and white stripes that our Swedish Queen Silvia wore at the Nobel Prize party in 1993. Nina Ricci designed that one.

I have a few striped dresses myself but none so glamorous as Sylvia's. These days I don't wear them, but I can't bear to give them away. But I do have many, many striped T-shirts.

My husband preferred T-shirts with goofy pictures and strange slogans and sayings. I especially remember two of his. One had a drawing of a big cow's head on it with the caption: "AMY THE ARMADILLO." The morose cow had a speech bubble over her head that said: "I am not an Armadillo." I could never understand what the cow had to do with the armadillo. Maybe he just wore the T-shirt to give people something to ponder. If you asked him to explain the meaning of the shirt, he would only give a secretive and cunning smile. His other favorite T-shirt simply said: "Beyond Repair." It was easier to understand but, for the wife of its wearer, harder to take. The statement seemed definitive somehow, but impossible to do anything about.

Some people subscribe to the idea that horizontal lines on one's clothing are fattening, while vertical lines are slimming. If I continue to eat so much chocolate I may need to move to wearing vertical striped shirts from the horizontal ones I prefer.

Marie Kondo is a Japanese woman who has known fame all over the world as an organizer and cleaning specialist for our homes. Her books have inspired many to get their lives in order, especially their wardrobes. She has inspired me. Among other things, she has propagated the idea for how to cleverly fold your clothes to store them in such a way that fits more of them into a drawer, while also allowing a better view of all your shirts.

In my wardrobe, the striped T-shirts fight for space. All of them are folded according to Marie Kondo's instructions, but if the drawer is full, it's full. In fact, I have two drawers of striped shirts. How did I collect so many striped shirts? A blue one with white stripes, a white one with red stripes, a yellow one with pink stripes, a green with white, and so on, and so on, and so on. My list of stripy shirt options is incredibly long and the combinations of stripes by colors sometimes seem endless when I open my organized drawers.

Perhaps I should will my stripy shirt collection to Jacob Dahlgren for his next work; perhaps he will be inspired. Perhaps I do have too many and should death clean those drawers.

But I remind myself that while stripes may not make you look young, they also do not make you look old and they always bring joy.

SURROUND YOURSELF WITH THE YOUNG(ER) OR *BUSVISSLA* TO YOUR YOUNGER SELF

When I left the launch party for my first book I was overjoyed. I was eighty-five years old and had just made my debut as an author. I asked my Swedish publisher, Abbe, how I was ever going to be able to thank him. He laughed and said:

"The only thing you need to do to thank me is this: always be kind to those younger than you."

Everyone is younger than me, so I have ample opportunity to practice this.

But it has been easy for me for other reasons. I've always had young people around me. Not just my five children, but also their kids and all the friends of my children and grandchildren.

When I moved to Stockholm from Gothenburg in 2006, my husband had just passed away. I was devastated but at the same time curious to rediscover the big city I had lived in as a twenty-year-old art student. My husband and I had lived for many years in a tiny community on an island off the west coast of Sweden. Now I was going to visit galleries again.

Stockholm took me in. I found new friends. It was so much fun. A young man—Ulrik—wanted to do a blog with me about art. Young people, children of my old friends and of my own children, came to dinner. It was really different from the life I had lived on the island. A life I had also liked.

As you get older, it is important to listen to the young. It can be a lot more fun and interesting than listening to eighty-somethings shaking their fists, waving their canes, and saying everything was better in the old days.

My father was a doctor. He specialized in gynecology and obstetrics. In the doorway of the apartment house where we lived, there was a gold plaque with his name and profession. For some reason, it provoked a reaction in some of the boys who escorted me home after a dance or a party. I don't think the plaque would have caused the same reaction if Dad had a flower shop or built houses; those professions would hardly have led to blushing or giggles. To me their reaction to the plaque became a sort of measuring stick for how immature young teenage boys could be. Today I think their reactions were simply a bit comical.

When I was a little girl, maybe five, six years old, my father took me on his Sunday rounds in the hospitals to check on his patients. While he was doing his consultations, I had to wait in the hallway. I used that time to walk around and look at what hung on the walls or lay in the glass

cabinets. There were some strange instruments and pros-
thetics on display, and sometimes the kind nurses would
stop and talk to me for a while, so it never got to be boring.

As soon as Father was done, we would go to one, sometimes two art galleries to look at paintings, drawings, and
the occasional sculpture. I loved seeing everything and I
learned a lot of things I've used throughout my whole life.
Coming to another country, to a new city, and visiting an
art museum only to recognize a painting or an artist's work
I had seen a long time ago with my father always feels like
meeting an old friend.

Every now and then on Sundays—unless it rained,
which happens quite a lot in Gothenburg—we went down
to the harbor. My dad loved taking pictures, especially if it
was a bit foggy, as that acted almost like a soft filter for his
camera. I still have some of his harbor photos tucked away.
Sometimes, if he managed to steal a few slices of bread
without our housekeeper, Mrs. Karlsson, noticing, he would
bring a bag of them or maybe just bread crumbs tucked in
his pocket. Mrs. Karlsson was our housekeeper, but I think
she was really our boss—even Dad was a bit intimidated by
her. My father and I used to think that she sometimes kept a
little too strict an eye on our household's inventory. But we
didn't want to unnecessarily provoke her, so we had to be
careful.

It didn't take long before seagulls and terns were cir-
cling us, and ducks were swimming toward us. It was fun
throwing bread to them, trying to aim so that everyone got
a piece. When the bag was empty, Daddy would bring it to
his mouth, take a giant breath, inflate it, and then quickly

pop it. *Bang!!!* Away the birds flew, making a terrible racket as their wings flapped. It was Sunday's climax. Afterward, we went home to eat lunch.

My father was an "old-school" doctor. If he had promised a woman he'd be there when her children wanted out into the world, he kept his promise, even if it meant leaving the table in the middle of Christmas dinner. I remember him actually doing that one time, but he was soon home again. Happy as a lark.

As I was awaiting my fifth child, my parents came to visit. At the time we lived a couple of kilometers outside Gothenburg. My husband, Lars, wasn't home and I was nine months pregnant. The baby was fully baked. A nanny, who was supposed to take care of the older children while I was in the hospital, was already there. I made some coffee and gingerbread cookies and we sat down to have a chat. Suddenly my dad, who kept a close eye on everything, says, "I think you are in pre-labor; maybe we ought to go to the hospital." I hate sitting and waiting; pacing back and forth in the hospital hallway was something I had done a lot of and I always wanted to stay at home for as long as possible, but nevertheless we went.

But first I had to inform the nanny. I told her she was free to invite her boyfriend over if she wanted company. I had met him; he was no monster. She blushed and said, "He is already here. He climbed through my window last night."

"Ok," I said (keeping an open mind). "Very well. Make sure he enters through the front door from now on. Eat together and play family for a couple of days. You'll have a great time."

Dad followed me to the delivery floor but was not allowed into the delivery room. Hardly half an hour later the baby was born, but the medical staff soon became concerned as unfortunately the placenta hadn't fully come out. I began to become concerned too. The doctor asked if I had eaten something recently and I told him a gingerbread cookie! He went on to pump my stomach. Damn that cookie! After that, I hardly ever have cookies.

The little girl, though, was a real beauty, so who cared about partially digested cookies in the end. She didn't have much hair, but she looked so pleased and made small, funny-sounding noises. Grandmother and grandfather came by again the next day to witness the miracle, and a telegram arrived from my husband on his way back from the USA. I was happy.

In speaking of happiness, I know what it is. Happiness is being surrounded by the young. My father knew it. I know it. And if you are over eighty, even a seventy-six-year-old is young. That, too, is happiness.

Of course, some people are idiots. Young or old. And I do not in any way want to say that young people are better than the old, or even more interesting or valuable. The thing with young people is that they lack experience, have new thoughts, have troubles and worries that most people my age have dealt with and gotten over. Surrounding yourself with young people is a way to stay in tune with the young person you yourself were at some point.

When I was young, I had great expectations. I was to become a world-famous painter. I would draw human longing; I would paint our souls. I would exhibit at the greatest galleries. Nothing would stop me.

When I hear young people talking about their dreams I am reminded of my young self, and also reminded that I am still the same person.

When I was young, there were three things I had always wanted to be able to do. They were: to play the trumpet, to tap-dance, and to *busvissla*—make the kind of extraloud whistle where you put your fingers in your mouth to amplify the sound. I don't know the English word. One of my daughters says it is close to a "wolf whistle," but not exactly—whatever it is, if you do it right, you can get anyone's attention.

I don't know why I have always wanted to do these

things. I think that some of the tasks are useful in unusual situations. Some are mostly just for the fun of it.

I knew a lady who was very elegant. One day we were out shopping in town. When we were ready, we wanted a cab to bring us home with our heavy packages. I could not believe my eyes, or my ears. The elegant lady did not wave her hand but emitted a clear and loud whistle—a *busvissla*. I was so impressed! Ever since I have tried to make that sound but without any result. I do not know why; maybe my lips, teeth, or tongue is not made for a *busvissel*.

To blow the trumpet is another way to make noise, but that was not the reason why I wanted to toot it myself. I really like trumpet music and loved to listen to Louis Armstrong, Bunny Berigan, and Harry James and others when I was young. I once borrowed a trumpet from a friend and tried to produce sounds from it. When my efforts did not produce any results at all, I gave it back. I told myself: to just listen is really much more enjoyable. And yet sometimes still I have the desire, the yearning, to make that noise.

Tap dance was popular in the thirties when I was born. My dad, who was a good dancer, could tap-dance. I never could, even when he tried to teach me as a small child. Tap-dancing was certainly a bit different from jitterbugging, which I did in Stockholm in the 1950s only twenty years later; jitterbugging I was able to do, maybe because I had a partner the same height in my beloved Lars.

Now I enjoy watching Fred Astaire and Ginger Rogers tap-dancing on YouTube and still have the desire to learn.

I have not yet given up. I think there is still hope. Maybe I will *busvissla* and tap-dance on my balcony one day. But I think I will spare my neighbors from trumpet blowing.

It is never too late to do anything, unless it really is too late and you are dead. The moment you start thinking it is too late, then you begin to die. I will keep going and do all I want to do. Maybe I'll have an art opening in New York. My father would have liked that.

APPENDIX: BONUS THOUGHTS AND TIPS ON DEATH CLEANING

HOW TO BROACH ONE OF LIFE'S MOST IMPORTANT TOPICS WITH YOUR LOVED ONES

As we age, many of us spend less time with our parents, and it can be hard to find a time to talk about death cleaning. During the holidays, many of us travel far and wide to reunite with brothers, sisters, and, above all, parents. Parents who, no matter how wonderful they are, are growing older. If you're unlucky, they are also the happy owners of a mountain of stuff, precious only to them. And guess who will have to eventually take care of all that stuff?

The holidays are that warm and lovely time of year when many of us consume more than we can handle. Presents, food, eggnog—it never stops. The days after the holidays are in fact a good time to talk about how much we consume in general, and about how many of us just have too much stuff. Maybe not on Christmas Eve per se, or your first visit home in a while—that would be a serious downer. But it is my experience that most families find the whole holiday experience exhausting, both financially and physically. This is something we can all relate to and talk about. Sit down and talk about the next holiday, whatever that holiday might be. In Sweden it is Midsummer. It might be Eid, Diwali, Purim; it could be a birth, wedding, adoption, funeral. The point is to talk.

Also, help your future self and make your parents truly happy: talk to them about what they want to do with all their stuff.

Writing my book on death cleaning helped my children and me talk about death in a constructive way. I have tried to make my approach fun and full of light. Talking and reading about difficult things always makes them easier. Death is a difficult topic, and we should really talk about it more.

Death is the toughest topic. Understandably. Death cleaning doesn't have to be: it's a very useful and practical approach to what can be a difficult or frightening topic. Whether you're middle-aged and facing your parents' passing, or thinking of your own, there is no moment better than the present to prepare for death. My goodness, we plan for everything. Why not death?

Death cleaning is not just for older people; I even think that people as young as forty can begin the process. If they continue regularly throughout their lives, they won't have so much to clean up when they are older and have less energy to do this demanding work.

For all the brave who start their own *döstädning*—I salute you! While you will make things easier for the people who come after you and life will be simpler for you, you will also discover that you have a good time doing it. It is a way to walk down your life's memory lane and see how the stories of your life weave together—as told through the things that you have kept—you will have a nice and thoughtful time.

When I was young, it was considered rude to speak your mind to an older person, including your own parents. Thankfully, today we generally believe that honesty is more important than politeness. At best, we combine the two. Talking about death cleaning can be a way for generations to talk to one another about what is important to them.

People often ask me how to approach the topic, how to even start the conversation. If your parents are getting old and you don't know how to bring up death cleaning, I would suggest paying them a visit, sitting them down, and asking the following questions in a gentle way:

"You have so many nice things; have you thought about what you want to do with it all later on?"

"Do you enjoy having all this stuff?"

"Could life be easier and less tiring if we got rid of some of this stuff that you have collected over the years?"

"Is there anything we slowly can do together so that you won't be overwhelmed later on by having to care for so much stuff?"

Old people often have balance issues. Rugs, stacks of books on the floor, and odd items lying about the house can be serious safety hazards. Perhaps this can be a way to start your discussion: Ask about the carpets. Are they really safe? Do they have to be there?

Perhaps this is where "tact" is still important, to ask these questions as gently and sensitively as you can. The first few times you bring up death cleaning, your parents may want to avoid the topic, or change the subject. If you are unable to get them to talk to you, give them a little time to think, then come back a few weeks or months later and ask again, perhaps with a slightly different angle.

Or ask them over the phone; mention that there are certain items in their house that you'd like to have and could you perhaps take them now? They might be relieved to get rid of a few things and finally see the promise and possible enjoyment of beginning to death clean for themselves. If you're too scared to appear "impolite" with your parents or startle them and you don't dare bring up death cleaning, then don't be surprised if you get stuck with it all later on!

Holiday time next year (or the year after, or year after). It's possible that your parents have passed away and you're going through the gifts you gave them last year. They really appreciated those gifts and held on to them. They also valued your conversation about their many possessions and started death cleaning. These lovely old people helped you all your life. Now they've helped you again. The attic is empty, the basement and garage too. They've given most of their stuff to charity, helping countless strangers in need, and some of the things you said you wanted they've kept and assigned to you with little notes. You loved these parents. You are sad that they are gone, but you do not miss all their stuff: you can cherish their memories, not cherish their *skräp* (Swedish for "junk")!

THE WORLD MAY ALWAYS BE ENDING, BUT SPRING CLEANING ALWAYS ARRIVES . . . UNTIL THE DAY IT DOESN'T

When spring is in the air, everything is lovely. Especially for those of us who live in countries with four seasons, it always feels as if it were years since we had a spring season.

We can hear birds chirping. They are not singing yet, but they will. We can see early spring flowers like winter aconite (*vintergäck*) and snowdrops popping up and the buds on trees are swelling.

Suddenly the sun seems to shine sharper than before and I realize that my windows are not as clean as I like them to be. Especially now that I've had my cataract operation, the streaks on my window are as shocking as the wrinkles I once saw in my mirror. The sun-highlighted streaks on my windows confirm for me that it is time for spring cleaning! Wow!

Maybe you have read about death cleaning? Maybe you have already started it. In that case, half of your work, perhaps even more, is already done, because you will have fewer things to dust and clean.

Anyway, I think there is something positive just in the word "spring-cleaning." Part of that is because you begin to remember the wonderful feeling when it is done. Spring will feel like it has arrived and your windows will sparkle, the world outside sunlight, bright and welcoming.

So let's get started:

1. Begin with the windows. With clean windowpanes it is easier to see the murkiest, forgotten areas inside your home.

2. Then go through clothes, fabrics like curtains, and smaller rugs. Air out, wash, or take out some items for dry cleaning. If you can dry your laundry outdoors, it will smell so fresh. And while you are at it, you may realize there were some things you never used during the winter months and which perhaps you can now get rid of. That will make next year's spring cleaning so much easier!

3. Dust and wipe all surfaces and shelves.

4. Vacuum-clean all soft furniture and pillows.

5. Vacuum-clean all floors and wash/mop them.

If you have a huge living space, you will need more than one day to get it all done, but for me today with my two-room apartment I can sit down and rest with a nice cup of tea or coffee and admire my work. Last, I will pick or buy some nice flowers and shout:

"Welcome, Spring!"

DEATH-CLEANING DISCOVERIES
IN THE TIME OF COVID
AND ANSWERS TO OTHER QUESTIONS
I HAVE RECEIVED FROM
CURIOUS NOVICE DEATH CLEANERS

You could be dead tomorrow. We all could—but should you really make others suffer because you were too lazy to sort your stuff, even during weeks or months of quarantine?

If you didn't death clean during the virus—what is your excuse?

1. PHOTOS: If you have too many photos, you can start by getting rid of those you regret that you ever took—be it because you no longer like the people in the picture, you look terrible, or you are covering the lens with your finger. After that, throw away all doubles. If you have thirty-four pictures from someone's party, wedding, or graduation, save three and send the rest to the person who was being celebrated or save the photos to give to them in person. It will brighten their day. Only save what your loved ones would like to look at.

2. KITCHEN CABINETS: Revisit your kitchen food cabinets now and then. Any food that has expired should be thrown out—but throwing out food is such a sad waste. Think about this when you shop. "Will I eat these lima beans? How about this extra-firm tofu? Or will it eventually end up being cleaned out?"

3. BOOKS: I still keep my favorite books on the bookshelf. I am rereading some that I had forgotten about and discovering I have a few new favorites, but the others I will pack up and give away maybe to charity, a secondhand bookstore, a library, a school, or a young person who loves to read.

4. LARGE FURNITURE: With all this done, you might have time to think about what is in the attic and garage—what can you get rid of—what to save, and please, have a look at your furniture. You probably wish to forget about all this, and you probably have, for twenty, thirty years. Now is the time to sort it out. Arm yourself with paper, pen, and Post-its and go to it. Thirty minutes a day is a good start. Work up to an hour a day. Reward yourself after every accomplishment: a nice coffee, a good cake, a warm shower or bath. If you hit three hours of death cleaning, I would suggest a cold beer.

5. TAKE NOTES: Have a notebook and pen in hand when you are going through your stuff. As you go through your belongings, you will get useful ideas. Of course, that little watercolor painting would be loved by an aunt or son. The binoculars would be perfect for Uncle Gustav, who is almost blind but still loves to go to the theater. With all the future gifts you find in your home, it will feel as if it were the night before Christmas. But if you do not write them down, you will forget your great gift ideas. You could even put a Post-it on each item with the recipient's name and a little thought about why this particular ceramic

piece feels perfect for one person, or that little rug to another and your porcelain cat to a third.

6. MAKEUP FROM THE SEVENTIES: When you have decided to get rid of the things you no longer need, it's not a good idea to just go dump it all in the garbage. Yes, it may be the easiest thing to do, the garbage is close by, but try to get rid of things in ways that also make you feel good about yourself and your tasks. Contact your municipality and ask how you should best deal with your stuff. Is there a recycling station? Or a place where you can leave the hazardous waste, i.e., leftover paint, broken glass, old makeup such as your frosted, shimmering light blue eye shadow, or shampoo from former centuries and anything else that is environmentally hazardous or that someone can injure themselves with?

7. PILLS: Go to the pharmacy with any pills or liquid medications that have been someone else's or your own, especially in cases where the expiration date has passed.

8. PERSONAL PAPERS: Unfortunately, as I write this, I do not think the pandemic has completely subsided. For the foreseeable future we should preferably not travel around unnecessarily and remain cautious about making new acquaintances. Instead it is a good opportunity to "visit" with old friends by going through all your old letters and even postcards that you saved. Enjoy your visits, but then run the letters and postcards through your shredder; it will

sound like music! If you do not have a shredder, scissors will do, or just rip stuff up with your hands as you walk around your living space to provide a little physical exercise. Perhaps all that physical activity will help you sharpen your memory of the contents and feelings in the letters without actually having to keep them around to collect dust.

9. SENTIMENTAL ITEMS: Many people say they want to get rid of things, particularly because of space issues, and yet they keep them because of the memories these items carry. And yet sometimes it really is the right time to let something go. If you have to get rid of an item you cherish, something full of memories, take a picture of it. Then let the thing go. You might say something to it as you part. Nothing ceremonial or difficult. Make it easy, just say, "Thank you, my dear."

All this will of course take time, and when you are finished with any remaining death cleaning, you can live happily for many years in your new uncluttered lifestyle. After all, death cleaning is mostly about getting organized, not dying.

In a way, I wish I hadn't been so efficient when I was first thinking about and writing my first book, as I did a lot of *döstadning* then. I now wish I had more death cleaning left to do.

But there is a benefit. Now I can sit around thinking a lot: What will happen next? Will we starve? Will there be a war? Will there be a depression? A daughter says:

"One day at a time, Mom."

A son says:

"Do not regret; do not worry."

If we have done our death cleaning, we will know that our kids and our loved ones have a few nice things from us and can spend nice evenings in the park, instead of spending them sorting through my cupboards and closets.

Get started, MM.

April 2020

Adapted from a piece published on Psychologytoday.com

ACKNOWLEDGMENTS

A warm thank-you to everyone who has made this book possible: Susanna Lea, Nan Graham, Kara Watson, and Abbe Bonnier!

Also, a super thank-you to Stephen Morrison for cheering me on all the way and for an abundance of ideas. Also, my kids, well "kids," some of them are above sixty by now, but thank you for making my life deep and funny, and thanks to Jane and Lars for being right next door.

ABOUT THE AUTHOR

Margareta Magnusson is, in her own words, aged between eighty and one hundred. Born in Sweden, she has lived all over the world. Margareta graduated from Beckmans College of Design and her art has been exhibited in galleries from Hong Kong to Singapore. She has five children and lives in Stockholm. She is also the author of *The Gentle Art of Swedish Death Cleaning*.